EXPERIENCING GOD'S PROMISES
IN COLOMBIAN TRENCHES

The Community of Hope

www.community-of-hope.org

149 S. Panama Street
Montggomery, AL. 36107
334.832.HOPE

EXPERIENCING GOD'S PROMISES
IN COLOMBIAN TRENCHES

WRITTEN BY
JIM OLIVER

Contents

One of the richest blessings we have as children of God is the abundance of awesome and precious promises our Heavenly Father has given us. For most Christians these are nothing more than familiar scripture verses, read and quoted for inspiration but never finding relevancy in our normal daily challenges. However, when one's faith is exercised to the point of accepting and applying these promises to our current situation, one readily discovers the faithfulness and power of a sovereign God who cares about every detail and need of our life.

Jim Oliver has written a beautiful testimony of a life based on the promises of God. He and his family had unusual challenges on the mission field in learning to claim these promises, but that walk of faith began much earlier. You will read of a hunger for God and a growing faith that came from believing the Word of God. You will identify with the practical needs and trials that are so common to life and of the victory that comes through believing God, even when the circumstances contradict every evidence of their trustworthiness.

You will be blessed as you read of a family who were obedient to God's call and used to plant churches and disciple new believers. Whether one is serving God on the mission field or through a secular vocation in America, it is evident that an effective witness and ministry comes from victorious faith being lived out in the daily routines of life. One earns a hearing for the gospel by a lifestyle of trusting God and becoming a channel of His promised power and blessing.

God's promises will become more relevant, and your faith will be strengthened as you read this book. I am confident you will discover a fullness of joy and more effective ministry, as Jim Oliver did, as you read his testimony of a life based firmly on the promises of God.

Jerry Rankin, President
International Mission Board, SBC

INTRODUCTION

HOW IT BEGAN

There are many publications in bookstores today that treat the promises of God, and several are well written. I examine these books closely since this is a favorite subject of mine, and to my surprise I have found that most treat the subject of the promises from a historical or theoretical point of view. That is good to a point, but if God's promises are to be taken seriously then someone must come forward and give us not just a list of the promises or the theory on how they may be applied, but also how the promises work in life today.   Can these promises that date back hundreds of years be success-fully applied in the Twentieth and Twenty-first Century? If so, by whom?

This is the purpose of this book: To give a live account of how God's promises have educated, inspired, protected, and given wisdom and direction to my family and me during the 39 years of full time service, most of which was served as missionaries in Colombia, South America. Colombia is a country that is known to be one of the most dangerous for citizen and foreigner alike, a country torn apart by internal strife and intimidated daily by drug cartels, bombings and kidnappings. This book is about living out the promises in Colombian trenches. My family and I can testify that God's promises work today as they have for centuries, beginning first with those who received them and continuing to the faithful of today. I believe you, while reading this book, will come to the same conclusion.

But some may ask, "Is a study of the promises important for Christian living today?" "Isn't just getting our foot in heaven's gate enough for the believer?" "Can't we commit the sin of presumption by asking God to fulfill these promises in our lives?" You will find answers to these questions in the sermons of Charles H. Spurgeon printed in the second part of this book and hopefully in our testimony as we have tried to live out the promises in daily life. Charles Spurgeon was a powerful preacher of the gospel and author in England during the nineteenth century. For years his sermons were printed in New York papers the day after he preached them, and his books have sold millions and are still popular today.

I would like to add another contemporary word about the need for knowing and living by God's promises today. Dr. John Piper, senior pastor of Bethlehem Baptist Church in Minneapolis, Minnesota led his church in a series of 14 sermons that had as their theme the promises of God. Here are a few points from two of his sermons preached September 11 and 18, 1988 that inaugurated this series:

> Belief in the promises of God is the root of all love and unbelief is the root of all sin and unlove. 1 Timothy 6:10 says, "the love of money is the root of all evil." But what is money? It is a symbol of human resources and when one loves money he has faith in it, worships it and says I will put my trust in it and not in God and his provisions. But Jesus said you cannot serve God and money. God's plan is as Isaiah 55:1 says, "Ho, every one that thirsteth, come ye to the waters, and he that hath no money; come ye, buy, and eat; yea, come, buy wine and milk without money and without price." Therefore, we must do as the author of Hebrews teaches when he says, "hold

fast the profession of our faith without wavering; for he is faithful that promised."

Paul states in Romans 4:19-21 that the manner in which we bring glory to God is by believing in his promises. Abraham was strong in faith, "giving glory to God." The greatest contempt to someone is to say "I can't trust you," but when we believe them (trust them and their word) we magnify, honor and rely upon their wisdom to help us.

This trust, according to 1 Thessalonians 1:3 and 2 Thessalonians 1:11, also teaches us that belief in God's promises produces the "work of faith and labour of love." Our battle to "keep the faith" is lifelong but this is "the victory that overcomes the world."

This book was not written to be read and put aside, but as a resource for the study of God's promises for you and your family. Let me encourage you to read with notebook and pencil at hand. Every time you come across a promise write it down; plead the promise in prayer (Is this promise for you or not?— I believe God will let you know); fulfil the condition if there is one; and trust God to bring it to fruition. Spurgeon says promises are like checks and if one comes to heaven's bank at the right date, he will receive the promised amount at once. If the date should happen to be further on, he must patiently wait until its arrival; but meanwhile he may count the promise as money, for the bank is sure to pay when the due date arrives. Remember, "He is faithful that promised." (Hebrews 10:23)

I

ACCORDING TO PROMISE

On November 30, 1967 my wife Marilyn and I and our four children arrived by ship at the city of Cartagena, Colombia. We were beginning our missionary career in Barranquilla, which was a three-hour drive from Cartagena. I had been appointed to serve as Field Missionary for two Departments of Colombia; Atlantico and Magdalena, and would work mainly in the two largest cities of Barranquilla and Santa Marta. Marilyn, a Registered Nurse, served some in our Baptist Clinic but was occupied mostly with her duties at home as mother and wife. She also played the piano for the choir and taught Sunday School at the Central Baptist Church. Our children were all happily enrolled in school.

During our second year on the field, a friend of mine, Rev. Arles Bingham, pastor of the Strongsville Baptist Church in Ohio, sent me a series of sermons titled "According To Promise." This little book contained 20 sermons by Charles H. Spurgeon that dealt with the theme of the promises of God. Besides the Bible, there has never been a book that has affected my life so much as this. After reading the book I ordered copies for all of our missionaries in Colombia and for your reference I have included these sermons in the second part of this book. Some inspirational points in his sermons that launched me into my study of the wealth I posess are also included here. Dr. Spurgeon said:

> My hope lies only in the promise of God. He has set forth that promise in the person of his Son Jesus to every sinner that believeth in him; and I do believe in him, therefore I trust and believe that the Lord will fulfil his promise and bless me. The Lord our God, who bids us believe, also enables us to believe. Hope, kindled by a divine promise, affects the entire life of a man in his inmost thoughts, ways and feelings: it may seem to be of less importance than correct moral deportment but in truth it is of vital moment, not only in itself, but in that which it produces upon the mind, heart and life. The secret hope of a man is a truer test of his conditions before God than the acts of any one day, or even the public devotions of a year. As a man's hopes are, such is he. If his hope is in the promise of God, it is, it must be, well with him.

He continues:

> The promise lights up our whole career and makes us truly blessed. God's smile beheld by faith gives us fullness of joy. Confidence in the Person involves confidence in all that he speaks: hence we accept all the promises of God as being sure and certain. We do not trust one promise and doubt another, but we rely upon each one as true, and we believe it is true to us so far as it has respect to our condition and circumstances. We argue from general statements to particular applications.

About the surety of God's promises Spurgeon says:

Shall the Lord God Almighty fail in his promise? No, he will move heaven and earth, and shake the universe, rather than be behind-hand with his word. He seems to say — 'It must be done. I have promised —- promised, do you hear?' Sooner than his promise should fail, he spared not his own Son. Better Jesus die than the word of the Lord be broken.

Charles Spurgeon tells why God gives promises:

Our tendency is to get away from a real God. We live and move in the region of materialism, and we are apt to be enthralled in its influences. These visible things (our bodies, the world and its crosses) are unsubstantial, but they appear sadly solid to us: what we need is to know the invisible to be quite as real as that which is seen, and even more so. We need a living God in this dying world. The Lord is training his people to perceive himself: the promise is part of this educational process. These promises which as yet are unfilled are precious helps to our advance in the spiritual life. We are encouraged by exceeding, great and precious promises to aspire to higher things. We read the promise, accept it by faith, plead it in prayer and in due season see it fulfilled. I think it well to repeat that we are put under the regime of promise in order that we may grow in faith. How could there be faith without a promise? How growing faith without grasping more and more of the promise.

Concerning the value of God's promises Dr. Spurgeon says:

Since the promises are our estate, let us form a correct estimate of our wealth; possibly we may not fully know how rich we are. It will be a pity to pine in poverty from ignorance of our large property. May the Holy Spirit help us to form a due valuation of the riches of grace and glory reserved for us in the covenant of promise.

Let me explain how this all began and continues to work out in my life. When I read these words about my great wealth it dawned on me I was ignorant of my large estate. I thought if one came to me and said I was now very wealthy because he had deposited in my bank account a large sum of money I would quickly rush to the bank and find out just how rich I was. I then asked myself why should I remain ignorant of my true wealth that was eternal and secure, not like mere money placed in a bank? I therefore resolved to know my true wealth. With Bible in hand I began at the first verse in Genesis and read every word, verse, chapter and book until I finished the last chapter of the Bible, Revelation 22. When I came upon a promise I first underlined it in my Bible and then wrote it in a notebook. When I finished my study, which took a year and a half, I took my notebook and wrote every promise and the verses it came from in my Promise Book. I found some promises were given only once in the Bible but more often than not there were several verses given for each promise. When I found a promise I would begin to pray, "Lord, is this a promise for me? If not, please let me know." Before I wrote the promise in my Promise Book I was convinced it was for me.

Before I began the study of my large estate I had heard that there were 30,000 promises in the Bible. There are 31,102 verses in the Bible and perhaps that is where the figure came from. I did not find 30,000 promises but I did find 305 specific, personal promises for my family and me. Since that time I have found other promises that I overlooked in my first study, and at this writing I count my real wealth at 324 promises.

Many Christians don't claim their wealth because they fear the sin of presumption. Satan tempted Jesus in this manner when he told him to cast himself from the pinnacle of the temple because God had promised to take care of him. I was glad to see that Charles Spurgeon treated this since this was a lingering fear in my heart also. He says: "There can never be presumption in humbly believing God; there may be a great deal of it in daring to question his word. We are not likely to err in trusting the promise too far. Our failure lies in want of faith, not in excess of it. It would be hard to believe God too much: it is dreadfully common to believe him too little. 'According to your faith be it unto you,' is a benediction from which the Lord will never draw back."

The more I understood about God's promises the more I realized that there are two common problems related to Christians not claiming their true wealth. First, there is an ignorance of God's promises. Second, where there is some knowledge, there is often a lack of the where-with-all to claim the promise. In other words, there is a lack of faith.

One of my responsibilities as I made this study was to travel to Santa Marta once a month and work with the pastor and church there. I enjoyed the work but one part of the trip was very depressing. Each time I drove to Santa Marta I had to pass over a narrow strip of land that divided the Caribbean Sea and a huge lake named *Cienaga Grande ("Big Marsh")*. The Sea and lake, as well as the beaches, were beautiful but the depressing part was the poverty of the people who lived there. Many homes were built of sticks with dirt floors and some even of plastic bags. The stomachs of many naked children were swollen due to malnutrition and many times, as I passed the area, I would see a funeral procession carrying a small wooden box to the cemetery to lay at rest a child whose life might have been spared in more prosperous surroundings. However, within a few steps of those living in poverty was one of the richest resources in the world, the Caribbean Sea. If the people living so near this immense wealth of minerals, fish, sunken treasures, etc., could only take advantage of it they would become the richest people in the world. But yet they lived in poverty. My question was why did they remain so poor while living so close to these riches? The answer is the same as why so many Christians never claim their wealth. The poor in Cienaga didn't know how to get the wealth from the sea. Or if they had some knowledge, they didn't have the where-with-all to do it.

After my year-and-a-half study of the promises I was drawn to the Living Bible for my daily devotions. It seemed the translators of this easy-to-read version of the Bible had a special attraction to God's promises. Here are some key verses that greatly inspired me to fully believe that what God had promised would become a reality in my life and that of my family. "God has given sacred promises; no wonder I exalt." (Psalm 108:7); "Never forget your promises to me your servant, for they are my only hope. They give me strength in all my troubles; how they refresh and revive me." (Psalm 119:49-50); "I stay awake through the night to think about your promises." (Psalm 119:148); "Every good thing the Lord had promised them came true." (Joshua 21:45); "And now, Lord God, do as you have promised concerning me and my family."

(2 Samuel 7:25); "The Lord's promise is sure. He speaks no careless word; all he says is purest truth, like silver seven times refined." (Psalm 12:6) "Friendship with God is reserved for those who reverence him. With them alone he shares the secrets of his promises." (Psalm 25:14)

Now let me show you some of my vast estate with the prayer that you will search the scriptures for your riches and may your motto be, "He staggered not at the promise of God through unbelief; but was strong in faith, giving glory to God: And being fully persuaded that, what he had promised he was also able to perform." (Romans 4:20-21)

II

THE MOST IMPORTANT PROMISE

Before me I have a sheet of paper; the first page of my Promise Book started over 30 years ago in Barranquilla, Colombia. It is yellow and wrinkled and torn with age, but the truth which is written on it is timeless. It says, "Salvation & Eternal Life for James C. Oliver, Jr." Below my name are these Bible references just as I wrote them: John 3:15-18, 36; 8:51; 11:25-26; 6:40; James 1:12 with an asterisk beside it (I don't remember why); 1 John 2:25; Psalm 37:40; Joel 2:32; Acts 2:12; Rom. 6:23; Rom. 10:9-10; 10:13, Mark 16:16; Titus 3:7 underlined in red (again I'm not sure why). Below these references I wrote John 3:15-18 both in English and Spanish.

This is my story. In the 1940's my parents bought a new two bedroom house in the neighborhood of Highland Gardens in Montgomery, Alabama when I was a young boy. My Dad, a chemical engineer, worked for the State Highway Department where he tested materials that were to be used in building highways and bridges in Alabama. Regular church attendance was not a habit for us.

One day a young pastor named Forrest Hicks visited our home and asked my mother if it was true that she played the piano. She said it was true. He then told her he was pastor of a new Baptist mission meeting in a home one block north of us and they had a piano but no one to play it. He asked if she would be their pianist. She said she wasn't a Baptist. He said it was okay with him that she wasn't a Baptist and if she would help them out he would greatly appreciate it. She consented and began playing regularly at the mission. My father spent most of his Sundays fishing at a nearby lake. I attended the mission a few times but usually went with Dad or stayed at home when mother went to church.

I had many fears during those years. I remember when we moved into our new home and my Dad gave me the choice of bedrooms. I thought if I chose the first bedroom, nearest the front door, someone might break in and kill me first. If I chose the back bedroom I would hear the commotion in the front room and escape out the window. I chose the back bedroom. My parents would sometimes argue, even violently. I vividly remember lying in bed at night during some of those arguments fearing one of my parents would kill the other and then kill me, the only witness. As I write this it seems almost comical but at that time in my life it was a very serious matter.

One Sunday morning, not long after mother began playing the piano at the mission, something happened that changed our lives. The pastor had finished preaching and asked the little congregation to sing a hymn of invitation, giving an opportunity for anyone to receive Christ by faith as his/her Savior and therefore accept the free gift of eternal life. Mother began playing the hymn but couldn't continue. She stopped (everyone continued to sing, I was told later), rose from her place, went to the pastor and told him she had never been a Christian but now was publicly receiving Christ as her Savior and desired to be baptized into the church.

I remember mother asking me to accompany her to her baptism on Sunday evening since dad would probably be away fishing. I reluctantly said I would. The baptism was held in the mother church, Capitol Heights Baptist, and I remember it as if it were yesterday. Just before mother went into the baptismal waters someone whispered to her that her husband had arrived and was sitting on the back pew in his fishing clothes. It was a very emotional moment: the picture of baptism portraying her new life in Christ, the presence of the two closest people of her life, husband and only son, the quiet music.

As mother was helped into the baptismal pool, everyone could see the tears that stained her cheeks. It was at that moment I realized I was a sinner, lost and away from God. Within my heart I received mother's Savior as mine, became faithful in Sunday School and worship attendance and later was baptized into the same church.

My father had been baptized as a young boy in the Daviston Baptist Church but had drifted far in sin. The Lord touched my Dad's heart that same night he did mine and he too returned to the Lord and his church. He was a charter member of the church along with mother and served in practically every office besides pastor. His disciplined study of the Sunday School prepared him to serve his own church and others in the Montgomery Baptist Association as the Sunday School promoter. Besides his work in the church and Association, Dad was also active in the Gideon organization and personally gave hundreds of New Testaments to new recruits at the Gunter Air Force Base near his home. There was also a noticeable change in our home life as we grew closer in love and acceptance. Mother served as pianist of the church until she died in 1974.

I can never express all that my new life in Christ has meant to me. One important thing is that he has helped me defeat fear; the proof of which came the day my wife, our four children and I were appointed to live and serve in Colombia,

South America, one of the most violent but beautiful nations on earth. One of God's promises was especially helpful. "Fear not: for I have redeemed thee, I have called thee by thy name; thou art mine. When thou passest through the waters, I will be with thee; and through the rivers, they shall not overflow thee: when thou walkest through the fire, thou shalt not be burned; neither shall the flame kindle upon thee. For I am the Lord thy God the Holy One of Israel." (Isaiah 43:1-3)

Every promise of mine is based on personal faith in Jesus Christ as my Lord and Saviour. The Bible teaches that "all the promises of God in him are yea, and in him Amen, unto the glory of God by us." (2 Corinthians 1:20) This means that the riches of God, his promises, are "yes" only to those who trust Jesus and are his disciples. There is only one promise given to the lost person, "Believe on the Lord Jesus Christ, and thou shalt be saved, and thy house." (Acts 16:31) That is not to say that God doesn't bless the unbeliever at times but these blessing are acts of his love to draw the lost to faith in Him. If you have never trusted Christ as your personal Savior, then I challenge you to open your heart to him in faith and begin claiming the great estate he has reserved for you in his promises. "He that believeth on the Son hath everlasting life: and he that be- lieveth not the Son shall not see life; but the wrath of God abideth on him." (John 3:36)

III

FINDING YOUR LIFE

When people consider the call to missionary service it is only natural to think about all the things they must give up. First, and probably the hardest of all, is the family. As they move to another country or very far away in their own land, they are confronted with many good-byes to family and friends. Mother and dad, grandparents, aunts, uncles, favorite cousins and later the separation of children as they leave home for school or to begin their family. It is no secret that family is the biggest reason missionaries resign and return home. All the above was difficult for us too, and then grandchildren came along and intensified the heartache even more. After separation from the family comes another anguish; loss of your native land and all the comforts that go with it. Most, if not all of us, love the country, state and town where we were born and raised. And if it was God's will that we be born in the greatest country in the world (some might disagree with this evaluation, but not many), why leave it to be a foreigner in a distant land? Add to this the difficulty of communication in a foreign tongue and you have a real problem that just won't go away. I have heard it said, and I believe it, that the language barrier is the second biggest reason missionaries "throw in the towel" and return home.

Another loss for some missionaries is that of a career. We had a pastor appointed to the English work in Bogota who told me he had larger Sunday School departments in his stateside church than the total membership of the Bogota Chapel. Was it a great surprise he returned to the states after one term? Missionary Wayne Wheeler once told me that while he was in the seminary, he had dreams of returning to Georgia, his native state, to pastor a fine church and maybe someday become president of the Georgia Baptist Convention. When his fiancee, Annette, announced she was called to foreign missions work he had to do a lot of praying and soul searching. Finally, he realized this was God's will for him and now after 30 plus years of fruitful service in Honduras and Panama he will happily tell you that becoming a missionary was one of the greatest decisions in his life.

Jesus said in Matthew 10:39, "He that findeth his life shall lose it: but he that loseth his life for my sake shall find it." Mark gives the same promise but adds, "whosoever shall lose his life for my sake and the gospel, the same shall save it." Here is one of many paradoxes found in the Bible and especially in the teachings of Jesus. When one lives for himself and his pleasures he virtually loses the abundant life with true and lasting joys. But when he gives his life to God (Jesus said "loses his life") then he finds true riches in this life as well as the life to come. In Matthew, as well as Mark and Luke, we find an interesting promise: "And every one that hath forsaken houses, or brethren, or sisters, or father, or mother, or wife, or children, or lands, for my name's sake, shall receive an hundredfold, and shall inherit everlasting life." (Matthew 19:29)

We consider our first term of missionary service not in Colombia but in Cleveland, Ohio. In the month of June, 1960, Marilyn, our son Dan and I packed up a U-Haul trailer and left a stable church position in a small sleepy town in Alabama to move north. I had been a summer missionary with the Home Mission Board after graduating from college in 1956 and had become close friends with Paul and Daisy Nevels who were serving as area missionaries for northeast Ohio and part of Pennsylvania and New York. The call to start Baptist Churches in Ohio was too strong for me to get away from, so after finishing seminary and a year's ministry in the solid south we returned to Ohio. Paul had kept us informed about the new work in his field and for several months had laid on our hearts a new neighborhood where 1200 new homes were being built each year and had only three churches, none of them Baptist. Brook Park, Ohio - what a challenge!

I vividly remember the feeling and thoughts I had as we left the state of Kentucky and drove across the bridge spanning the mighty Ohio river and entered a land of opportunity and promise. I thought of Abraham leaving the land of Ur, not knowing where he was going but fully trusting God had called him and would accompany him on all his journey for the rest of his life. I was leaving an established church, a good salary, a Baptist town in the state where I was born and raised and moving to a huge city and a church that didn't have one member. The Home Mission Board's policy for pioneer mission work at that time was to only help a constituted church when they were ready to pay a full-time pastor by giving them a small supplement for a period of 12 months. We had no church nor established mission so therefore could expect no financial help from the HMB.

Our first night in Cleveland was spent with Paul and Daisy and the next day Paul presented me with "my church," a stack of prospect cards. He said, "Jim, the summer missionaries have just finished two weeks of a religious survey in Brook Park and this is what they found." With his typical enthusiasm he thrust the treasure into my hand. "I have found a meeting place in the elementary school which is in the heart of the community and since they needed a name for the contract I took the liberty of naming your church. You are the pastor of The First Baptist Church, Brook Park. How do you like it?" What could I say? One day on the field and I was already pastor of First Baptist Church, at least pastor of some prospects who might be members of the church some day.

Paul continued, "I contracted the first service to be in two weeks so we have some time to round up the people to start your new work." With Paul's enthusiasm and the Lord's help I figured we could fill the elementary school auditorium for the first service. After all, we did have two full weeks to find and enlist the prospects. The two weeks passed very fast but many key prospects were visited and most gave fervent promises they would be in the first service. The big day arrived and on a bright and sunny Sunday morning in the middle of June the First Baptist Church (officially a mission) held its first meeting with thirteen people present, not including the summer workers.

The preacher's wife always gets the hardest jobs so during the first service Marilyn was off in another room "teaching" the children while I preached to the congregation of seven adults. After the sermon I gave the invitation to join the new church either by baptism, letter or statement and when I stepped around the pulpit I said this signified Marilyn and I were joining the church. I wanted to make sure no one beat me to the draw and joined first! We started the invitational hymn and all present joined the church on the first stanza. I made the announcement that since all who were present had joined, I saw no need to sing another stanza. We sat down and elected a treasurer, made plans for outreach visitation, had a prayer and went home. We were finally off and running and it was an exciting time.

That week I began looking for secular work since there would be no church salary for months, maybe longer. For five weeks I looked for employment but with no results, and as meager savings dwindled, anxious moments increased. While attending the seminary in Louisville, Kentucky I had a job working in a Firestone store operated by a dedicated Christian couple. During some of our visits in Brook Park I was happy to find a Firestone warehouse in our area that shipped merchandise to all of their stores in the Southeast. Maybe this would be our meal ticket until the church could put us on salary. During the interview with the manager I noticed he took particular interest in the fact that I was a pastor trying to start a Baptist church in Brook Park. Weeks went by with no response from Firestone and in the meantime I got a job selling Singer sewing machines in a store in the heart of Cleveland. The job at Singer didn't pay much and it was time-consuming in many ways, especially on Saturday, which was my most fruitful day of visitation for the church. I had been at Singer only a short time before I got a call from Firestone asking if I wanted the job. It was the perfect secular job for several reasons. It was near our apartment, the pay was stable - unlike commissions at Singer - and best of all I had Saturday and Sundays off.

Soon after I began working at Firestone I was introduced to a young man who had recently become a Christian. He was excited about his faith and took witnessing for the Lord very seriously, so much so that he neglected his work and caused other workers to do the same. When I first saw this I was amazed the manager would hire another preacher. I soon became close to my new brother in Christ and one day spoke to him about the neglect of his job and interference of the other men as they tried to work. I suggested we begin a Bible study during our lunch break and use our free time in witnessing but at the same time be honest to our employer by giving him a full day's work for a day's wages. I was happy my brother took my advice and became a faithful employee as well as an obedient witness. I worked at Firestone for the remainder of the year but was laid off after Christmas. The church was now strong enough to give us a living wage and when Firestone called me back in the Spring I declined because I could now give full time to my calling, the building of the church.

The call to start a new church presented a new adventure almost everyday. One of the difficult and challenging jobs we faced was constructing our own place of worship. Our members were mostly laborers and therefore limited in material resources. Most were buying their first home and expenses often exceeded income. Almost every member was a new Christian and had no training in the Biblical teachings of the tithe and offerings. They were maturing in their faith but it was a slow process. My home pastor, R.E. McKee, of the Highland Gardens Baptist Church in Montgomery gave us a lot of help which included underwriting our loan program and buying the first $10,000 worth of church bonds. This allowed us to buy three acres of land and draw plans for the first building. A few members bought enough bonds to build the walls but after that we were broke. We feared we might go through the winter with only four bare walls standing on the property. Near the end of the year I received a letter from a former summer missionary, Jerry Don Reynolds, with a check for a thousand dollars and two one hundred dollar bills enclosed. This was enough to put on the roof but a hard winter was approaching and we had no more funds to finish the building.

"Preacher, what we gonna do?" asked one of my West Virginia members. "The payment on the bonds we sold earlier will be higher in a few months and we will still be in the school paying rent." That wasn't anything new to me but what were we going to do? As Christmas approached we were a very discouraged body of believers.

One day I said to Marilyn that it might be a good idea to return to Alabama and contact family and friends to see if they might be interested in buying more church bonds from us. The members thought it was a good idea also and voted for us to make the trip. That put some more excitement in our lives; we were heading home, at least for a few days.

Back in Alabama I made the rounds to all the possible buyers of our bonds but with very little success. Time was running out and soon we would have to return to Brook Park. Two days before we were to go back to Ohio I was traveling alone to Montgomery from an unsuccessful trip to the small town of Alex City and was approaching Kowliga bridge that spans beautiful Lake Martin, the recreational capital of central Alabama. I had just driven on the bridge when I had the impression someone was in the car with me. Though surprised, I didn't experience fear but at the same time I definitely felt this was no friend. I didn't feel threatened and was actually at ease to communicate with whoever was there. As I reflect on this incident today I believe I had an encounter, not with a lesser evil spirit as has often been my experience, but with Satan himself. His remarks, though not audible to human ears, were clearly understood and smooth.

I could now see the vast expanse of the lake when I heard a delicate voice, "Look over to your left, Jim. What's out there?"

I didn't need to think long before answering, "The home of my uncle Norman and aunt Nell."

After a pause he asked his second question, "What else is there?"

"My uncle Sebron and aunt Martha have a fishing cabin there," I answered.

Now he spoke with more feeling, "Jim, you're having a hard time in Ohio. Your church can't be finished because the people aren't behind you; they don't have money to give. Besides, you were raised in the south and don't like the cold, north winters." After a pause the voice continued. "Jim, your dad said he had a job for you in Montgomery. Why don't you forget Ohio, return to Alabama, your state, and enjoy this beautiful lake. You like fishing and camping and you have the perfect set-up for that here. Let your parents be with their grandchildren; come back home to your family."

I was now alone with my thoughts and a powerful temptation to leave Ohio and the new church and return to Alabama. The power to win this battle didn't come from me but from the Lord Jesus Christ, the same God that allowed Abraham and other disciples to win over their temptations and adversaries. We did return to our little church in Ohio. The members themselves bought enough bonds to finish the building and we moved into it the following summer. I thank God for the strength he gave me to return to the task. Since that day I have seen his hand in the establishment and ongoing growth of the First Baptist Church, Brook Park (now named Park Heights Baptist). I have served other churches in the United States for 8 years and have been a foreign missionary in Colombia for almost thirty years. Marilyn and I have reached retirement age now and we thank God for the victory over Satan at Kowliga bridge, Lake Martin, Christmas 1961.

Christian fellowship has meant a lot to us wherever we served. Fellowship with the missionary family in Colombia took on special meaning soon after arriving on the field and was lived out daily as we referred to one another as brother or sister and our children addressed other missionaries as aunts and uncles. It wasn't long before this family was enlarged with native Christians and today we literally have hundreds of brothers, sisters, fathers and mothers in the Lord. A bittersweet day for Marilyn and me was June 6, 1997, the day we left Colombia for the last time. Many Colombian brothers and sisters, along with the Brian Massey family, the new missionary couple in Cartagena, met us at the airport to bid farewell. Before boarding the plane we held hands, sang praises to God and prayed. We wept as we left Colombian soil because we knew we were leaving part of our precious family that God had graciously given to us during our years of service. We are happy to be back in our native land again because we are near our children and their families along with aunts, uncles and other kin. We have experienced the best of two worlds: our blood relatives and our Christian family in the

Lord. Our parents were promoted to heaven while we were in Colombia.

I never felt I gave up a career when I went to Colombia. Jesus said, "But as many that are first shall be last; and the last shall be first." (Matthew 19:30) A promise of God found in Deuteronomy 28:13 says, "And the Lord shall make thee the head, and not the tail; and thou shalt be above only, and thou shall not be beneath; if that thou hearken unto the commandments of the Lord thy God, which I command thee this day, to observe and to do them." I never dreamed of being a seminary professor but I had that opportunity for ten years at the International Baptist Seminary in Cali. Many were more prepared than I for that position but I believe the Lord placed me there for his purpose. Marilyn was also very happy in Cali as she served as secretary and station treasurer. Being elected president of the Colombian Baptist Mission is more work than honor but our colleagues elected me to that position for two terms and I am grateful I had the opportunity to serve them in that unique capacity. The Lord has given us a wonderful life as missionaries and neither Marilyn nor I would have swapped it for any other career. Praise God from whom all blessings flow!

IV

ABUNDANT LIFE

As you read the Bible you cannot help but be impressed by God's concern with our physical life on earth. After all, this is our training ground for heaven. I was greatly impressed by the sheer number of promises for our physical life. One of the first was found, of all places, in the Ten Commandments. Exodus 20:12 says, "Honour thy father and thy mother: that thy days may be long upon the land which the Lord thy God giveth thee." Deuteronomy 5:16 and Ephesians 6:2-3 repeat the same promise but add, "that it may be well with thee." Deuteronomy 11:8-9 gives the promise of a long life but with another condition besides honoring mother and father. Psalm 91:12 says, "With long life will I satisfy him, and show him my salvation."

Not all promises have conditions, though most do. The condition for this promise is to honor your earthly father and mother and the promise of God is a long life. It doesn't take much intelligence to know that not all godly people could claim this promise, the most famous of which was our Savior himself. What is the problem, if you want to call it that? Are these godly people ignorant of this promise? If they know it, do they lack honor toward their parents? If they know the promise and honor their parents do they lack the faith to claim the promise?   Of course we know, in the example of Jesus, the answer to all these questions is an emphatic NO! Then why did this promise not apply to Jesus as well as literally thousands, perhaps millions, of deeply spiritual Christians that died in their youth, most not being able to say (humanly speaking) that it was well with them?

The answer to that question, I believe, is that in their early death there was more to be gained for God's glory and the advancement of his kingdom and for themselves than to live a long life on earth. Not only "when the fullness of the time was come, God sent forth his Son," but also in the fullness of time he died for our sins and returned to the Heavenly Father. Jesus told his disciples, "It is expedient for you that I go away: for if I go not away, the Comforter will not come unto you; but if I depart, I will send him unto you." The human nature of Jesus agonized over his early death on the cross but he was able to say "nevertheless not as I will, but as thou wilt."

The blood of the martyrs has truly been for the glory of God and seed for the expansion of his kingdom. As it was in the past so is it today. The death of the five young missionaries at the hands of the Auca Indians in the jungles of Ecuador in 1954 seemed at first to be a great defeat by Satan, but in time it has proved to be a majestic act of love and faithfulness witnessed by all the world. Great gains in God's kingdom are still being seen as the result of this sacrifice as this once pagan tribe has been converted to the Lord. Many young people are continually inspired by the story of these missionaries to carry the gospel around the world.

In this matter of the promise of a long life I am at peace. If it is his will for me to go home sooner then I am ready, I say with Paul "to die is gain." However, I am also ready to live for him and my goal is the same as Paul, "for to me to live is Christ." I have asked for this promise in prayer, fulfilled its conditions as well as I know how and I believe with all my heart God will bring it to pass in my life.

I realize there is the danger of presumptuous sin related to this promise. God has so willed that I have a part in my physical health and if I neglect this responsibility then it would be similar to throwing myself from the pinnacle of the temple and asking God to protect me since he has promised do so. I must practice good eating habits, keep myself in shape physically, get proper rest and recreation, and refrain from any habit that could harm my health.

A long life, just in itself, may not be a blessing. Many have longed for death to take them from a life of physical or emotional suffering. Because of this some have gone to the extreme of taking their own lives. God knew a long life in itself wasn't enough for his children so he added more promises to give us not only "life" but a joyful, abundant and fruitful life. One of the most beautiful promises in the Bible given by Jesus is John 10:10, "The thief cometh not but for to steal, and to kill, and to destroy: I am come that they might have life, and that they might have it more abundantly." Many have tried to describe the abundant life Jesus promised but they continually fall short. Let me add, at this point, a few attributes of this abundant life as I see it but confess at the same time that what I say will only be the tip of the iceberg.

Jesus said in John 8:31-32, "If ye continue in my word, then are ye my disciples indeed; and ye shall know the truth, and the truth shall make you free." The truth that God loves all people regardless of race, nationality, education or social status has helped me in the struggle over prejudice. That hasn't been easy especially for one growing up in the deep south during the 40's and 50's. Unfortunately, I have seen the sin of prejudice raise its ugly head in other places in America as well as in other nations. Nevertheless, those still chained to prejudice are not free to live the abundant life in Christ. This promise also includes such things as freedom from inferior as well as superior attitudes, freedom to forgive others, freedom from fear and harmful habits as well as freedom from profane lifestyles which are condemned in God's word.

The Apostle Peter says, "Whereby are given unto us exceeding, great and precious promises: that by these ye might be partakers of the divine nature, having escaped the corruption that is in the world through lust." (2 Peter 1:4) Promises are given so we may first have Christ within us (partakers of the divine nature) and conquer sin in our lives (escape the corruption in the world). My tour of duty in the Army during the Korean Conflict and life in two foreign countries provided many temptations for almost every known sin, and though I can't say I've lived a perfect life, I can say God gave me the victory over any habitual or debilitating sin. Two special promises helped me in this battle for escaping this worldly corruption. One was James 4:7, "Resist the devil, and he will flee from you." The other was 1 Corinthians 10:13, "There hath no temptation taken you but such as is common to man; but God is faithful, who will not suffer you to be tempted above that ye are able; but will with the temptation also make a way to escape, that ye may be able to bear it." (Here is one of the few promises without a condition.) No one has or ever will experience the abundant life if habitual sin has not been conquered in his life. Christ has the power to free you from any evil habit by giving you strength to escape or bear up under the pressures of Satan's temptations.

We must be quick to say that we all are still sinners, but God has promised to forgive us and cleanse us if we confess our sins to him. 1 John 1:9 says, "If we confess our sins, he is faithful and just to forgive us our sins, and to cleanse us from all unrighteousness." I will always remember the day I was released from active duty from the U.S. Army. I sang all the way home after driving out of the main gate at Ft. Benning, Georgia because I was a free man, free from the Army. However, nothing can compare to the feeling I have when I think about the freedom I have in Christ over sin and the forgiveness I experience in my daily walk and confessions to him.

Does God give promises concerning the spiritual wellbeing of our children? Read these verses carefully and answer for yourself:

"For the promise is unto you, and to your children, and to all that are afar off, even as many as the Lord our God shall call." (Acts 2:39)

"But you must keep on believing the things you have been taught. You know they are true for you know that you can trust those of us who have taught you. You know how, when you were a small child, you were taught the holy Scriptures; and it is these that make you wise to accept God's salvation by trusting in Christ Jesus." (2 Timothy 3:14, 15) (Living Bible)

"Your sons hasten back, and those who lay waste depart from you. Lift up your eyes and look around; all your sons gather and come to you. As surely as I live, declares the Lord, you will wear them all as ornaments; you will put them on, like a bride. I will contend with those who contend with you, and your children I will save." (Isaiah 49:17-18, 25(b)) (NIV)

The hard fact for many Christian parents is that these promises are sometimes slow in coming and, unfortunately, some are convinced they will never come. Many have children living outside of God's will and bring shame on themselves and their family. I wish with all my heart this was not true for our children but I must be honest and say otherwise. Most of our children are married and have children and are active in worship and service to the Lord. However, one is living in open rebellion to God's word.

Words cannot express the grief this has brought upon his mother and me. The Bible is very clear about habitual sin and the eternal consequences for those who continue in this rebellion against God and his word. (Revelation 20:11-15).

Marilyn and I have tried to understand who is to blame; what we as parents did wrong or did not do that we should have done, but we realized such thoughts would not help us today. As parents we have repented of our sins related to this but we have also decided not to give up. God loves our children more than we do and he hasn't given up on any of them. The end of this matter has yet to be determined and until that day we fight the enemy primarily with four weapons: PRAYER. These promises are powerful and you will find them included in chapter seven. FAITH. As we have already seen this is a must in claiming God's promises. HOPE. This spark is within our heart that says, "one day all our children will return to God." LOVE. We often express our love to our children in spirit and deed and will continue to do so until our dying day.

I purposely placed this dark hour in our lives before the promises of joy because Christ's joy within us does not depend upon outward circumstances or how we are treated. It depends only upon our relationship to God. It is amazing how often joy is found in the Bible. The abundant life is filled with Christ's joy. A few of my "Joy" treasures are: Nehemiah 8:10, ".... Go your way, eat the fat, and drink the sweet, and send portions unto them for whom nothing is prepared; for this day is holy unto the Lord; neither be ye sorry; for the joy of the Lord is your strength."

"Thou wilt shew me the path of life; in thy presence is fullness of joy; at thy right hand there are pleasures for evermore." (Psalm 16:11)

"Weeping may endure for the night but joy cometh in the morning." (Psalm 30:5)

"Therefore with joy shall ye draw out of the wells of salvation." (Isaiah 12:3)

"These things have I spoken unto you, that my joy might remain in you and your joy might be full." (John 15:11)

"And these things write we unto you, that your joy may be full." (1 John 1:4)

An inspiration that helps me live the joyous life in Christ is John Piper's book, *Desiring God: Meditations Of A Christian Hedonist*. Read it. You will be blessed.

I summarize this section of joy and the problem of our child by saying:

- ◆ Marilyn and I will continue to love and serve the Lord to the best of our abilities.

- ◆ We will continue to love all of our family and help them when possible.

- ◆ We will continue to be joyful in our hearts.

- ◆ We will continue to "ask, seek and knock" at God's door until the final answer comes.

- ◆ We will continue to believe what the Lord has promised will be fulfilled in his time.

- ◆ We will continue to follow the teachings of Paul in Philippians 4:4-8. "Rejoice in the Lord alway: and again I say Rejoice. Let your moderation be known unto all men. The Lord is at hand. Be careful for nothing (don't be anxious); but in everything by prayer and supplication with thanksgiving let your requests be made known unto God. And the peace of God, which passeth all understanding, shall keep your hearts and minds through Christ Jesus. Finally, brothern, whatsoever things are true, whatsoever things are honest, whatsoever things are just, whatsoever things are pure, whatsoever things are lovely, whatsoever things are of good report; if there be any virtue, and if there be any praise, think on these things."

The paths of God's abundant life for us lead in many diverse directions. Psalms 34:10, says "The young lions do lack, and suffer hunger: but they that seek the Lord shall not want any good thing."

Psalm 84:11, "For the Lord God is a sun and shield: the Lord will give grace and glory: no good thing will he withhold from them that walk uprightly."

Think about these promises. There are no limits to God's

resources, and he has promised to shower his children whom he dearly loves with blessing upon blessing. Amazing!

The Andes mountains of Colombia are tall and majestic and I had many opportunities to see them by car, plane and on foot. When I was climbing these mountains either for pleasure or to share the gospel I was keenly aware of the promise found in Habakkuk 3:19, "The Lord God is my strength, and he will make my feet hinds' feet, and he will make me to walk upon mine high places." I have walked on high places with confidence and effectiveness in ministry because of his promise to me.

I began this chapter with the promise of a long life and now I will end it with a promise also related to life and health. Exodus 15:26 says, "If thou wilt diligently hearken to the voice of the Lord thy God, and wilt do that which is right in his sight, and will give ear to his commandments, and keep all his statutes, I will put none of these diseases upon thee, which I brought upon the Egyptians: for I am the Lord that healeth thee." (See also Deuteronomy 7:15). Years ago a hospital chaplain gave me the book entitled *None of These Diseases*, written by McMillen, M.D. This missionary physician inspires us to live by God's precepts by documenting how this promise of healthy living has worked out for many people and can work out in our lives as well. Jesus asked a sick man, "Do you want to be made well?" Another good question is, "Do you want to live a wholesome, healthy life?" Dr. McMillen says it is possible by believing and following God's word. I am happy to say this has been my experience through 66 years and by the grace of God I am pressing forward to even better days ahead. Charles Spurgeon says, "The promise of God is our best ground of assurance; it is far more sure than dreams and visions, and fancied revelations; and it is far to be trusted than feelings, either of joy or sorrow." With the psalmist I can say, "The boundary lines have fallen for me in pleasant places; surely I have a delightful inheritance." (Psalm 16:6) (NIV)

V

MATERIAL BLESSINGS

Charles Spurgeon, as the Bible, has much to say about our material needs. He says:

> He who is gone to prepare heaven for us will not leave us without provision for the journey thither. God does not give us heaven as the Pope gave England to the Spanish King - if he could get it: but he makes the road sure, as well as the end. Now, our earthly necessities are as real as our spiritual ones, and we may rest sure that the Lord will supply them. He will send us those supplies in the way of promise, prayer and faith, and so make them means of education for us. He will fit us for Canna by the experience of the wilderness.

He continues:

> My faith not only flies to heaven, but walks with God below; to me are all things daily given, while passing to and fro. The promise speaks of

worlds above, but not of these alone; it feeds and clothes me now with love, and makes this world my own. I trust the Lord, and he replies, in things both great and small. He honours faith with prompt supplies; faith honours him in all.

The Old Testament speaks of our material blessings: "If ye walk in my statutes, and keep my commandments, and do them; Then I will give you rain in due season, and the land shall yield her increase, and the trees of the field shall yield their fruit. And your threshing shall reach into the vintage and the vintage shall reach unto the sowing time: and ye shall eat your bread to the full and dwell in your land safely." (Leviticus 26:3-5)

Psalm 112:3 says "Wealth and riches shall be in his house (see verse 1 for the condition): and his righteousness endureth forever."

"The liberal shall be made fat: and he that watereth shall be watered also himself." (Proverbs 11:25)

Proverbs 3:9,10 have the same condition and wonderful promise. Proverbs says "Honour the Lord with thy substance and with the first fruits of all thine increase: So shall thy barns be filled with plenty and thy presses shall burst out with new wine." Malachi says that we should test God's promise when he says: "Bring ye all the tithes into the storehouse, that there may be meat in mine house and prove me herewith, saith the Lord of hosts, if I will not open you the windows of heaven, and pour you out a blessing, that there shall not be room enough to receive it." (3:10)

From the beginning of our marriage Marilyn and I made a commitment to tithe. We didn't do it because we felt it was the law nor did we tithe in order to get material blessings. We did it because we felt it was God's will for us. We did it voluntarily as Abraham did to Melchizedek, the priest of the most high God. If the Jews tithed because it was the Law couldn't we at least give the tenth under grace? There were times in our home when it wasn't easy to give the tithe but we both insisted it was right so we have been able to stick with it these 40 plus years. And has God blessed! There isn't room here to tell all the ways he has blessed in all areas of our lives: spiritual, material, mental, social, and his blessings continue day after day. Praise God from whom all blessings flow.

The New Testament didn't diminish the material promises but built upon them to bring us even greater blessings. Jesus made it very clear in the Sermon on the Mount that the physical needs of his disciples would be met. He amply treats this in Matthew 6:25-33 and sums up the lesson up in verses 31-33: "Therefore take no thought saying, What shall we eat? or What shall we drink? or Wherewithal shall we be clothed? (For after all these things do the Gentiles seek:) for your heavenly Father knoweth that ye have need of all these things. But seek ye first the kingdom of God, and his righteousness; and all these things shall be added unto you."

Here Jesus is saying if we, his children, meet the condition, "seek first the kingdom of God and his righteousness", then all our earthly needs will be supplied. Spurgeon has an important word about conditions to promises. He says:

> Certain covenant engagements, made with the Lord Jesus Christ, as to his elect and redeemed ones, are altogether without condition so far as we are concerned; but many other wealthy words of the Lord contain stipulations which must be carefully regarded, or we shall not obtain the blessing. One part of my reader's diligent search must be directed towards this most important point. God will keep his promise to thee; only see thou to it that the way in which the conditions are carefully observed of thee. Only when we fulfil the requirements of a conditional promise can we expect that promise to be fulfilled to us. In some cases, great blessedness is not realized because known duties are neglected. Do not

> undervalue the grace of the promise because it has a condition appended to it; for, as a rule, it is in this way made doubly valuable, — the condition being in itself another blessing, which the Lord has purposely made inseparable from that which thou desirest, that thou mayest gain two mercies while seeking only one.

The promise of Jesus concerning our needs being met is, without doubt, a case where the condition is really a greater blessing than the promise itself. Without minimizing our Lord's promise we can also say that material things cannot compare to seeking the kingdom of God and his righteousness. We rejoice that our physical needs are met, but what greater blessings we experience as we seek first his kingdom and his righteousness! The Apostle Paul saw this also and said, "For the kingdom of God is not meat and drink; but righteousness and peace, and joy in the Holy Spirit." (Romans 14:17)

God blesses us twice with a promise. First with the condition and then the fulfillment of the promised blessing. And as is often the case, the condition is an even greater blessing. There have been times when there was very little money in the bank or in our pockets but I can truthfully say neither I nor our family have gone without the necessities of life. Besides that, I have found joy and peace beyond words as I seek first the kingdom of God and his righteousness.

The Holy Spirit gave to the Apostle Paul this spiritual principle of giving and material possessions: "But this I say, he which soweth sparingly shall reap also sparingly; and he which soweth bountifully shall reap also bountifully. Every man according as he purposeth in his heart, so let him give; not grudgingly, or of necessity: for God loveth a cheerful giver. And God is able to make all grace abound toward you; that ye, always having sufficiency in all things, may abound in every good work." (2 Corinthians 9:6-8) The Living Bible gives this translation to verse 8: "God is able to make it up to you by giving everything you need and more, so that there will not only be enough for your own needs, but plenty left over to give joyfully to others."

Jesus says it beautifully in Luke 6:38, "Give, and it shall be given unto you; good measure, pressed down, and shaken together, and running over, shall men give into your bosom. For with the same measure that ye mete withal it shall be measured to you again." Around the middle of our missionary career in Colombia, Marilyn and I came to the conclusion that 10% of our income wasn't enough for the Lord and his work. We decided to increase our giving by 2% a year until we reached 25%. I don't say this for any vain glory because I realize, first of all, this is really a small percentage compared to what many are giving and second this is a small amount in comparison to his gifts to us. This 15% over and above our tithe has freed us to give to many good causes in the Lord's work such as help for mission property and equipment, evangelism materials for soul winners, specific needs among God's people and so on. God has richly blessed us and we, as Abraham was told, should be a blessing to others.

A word of warning must be sounded here. Material wealth can lead to avarice which is a snare in the lives of many people of the world and unfortunately, sometimes in the lives of Christians. Before Jesus gave the promise of our needs being met he warned against this trap into which many people fall. He said, "Lay not up for yourselves treasures upon earth, where moth and rust doth corrupt, and where thieves break through and steal: But lay up for yourselves treasures in heaven, where neither moth nor rust doth corrupt, and where thieves do not break through nor steal: For where your treasure is, there will your heart be also." (Matthew 6:19-20) In this same chapter in verse 24 he says, "Ye cannot serve God and mammon (money, material possessions)." God will bless us with material needs as we follow him but we must be very careful to keep them in proper perspective.

VI

PROMISED ANGELS

There are a lot of things about angels I don't understand but there is no doubt in my mind that they have been active in my life and around my family. One of the earlier accounts of angels is found in the life of Moses and the Hebrew children and is recorded in the book of Exodus. God said, "Behold, I send an Angel before thee in the way, and to bring thee into the place which I have prepared." (Exodus 23:20) Here is a promise of guidance and protection by one of God's special messengers called angels. It is interesting that God was already fulfilling this promise even before it was given. In Exodus 14:19 we find, "And the Angel of God, which went before the camp of Israel, removed and went behind them; and the pillar of the cloud went from before their face, and stood behind them." How glorious it is that God sometimes fulfills his promise even before he gives it.

Two key promises for me related to angels are found in Psalm 91:11, "For he shall give his angels charge over thee, to keep thee in all thy ways"; and Hebrews 1:13-14, "But to which of the angels said he at any time, sit on my right hand, until I make thine enemies thy footstool? Are they not all ministering spirits, sent forth to minister for them who shall be heirs of salvation."   There were many times I felt guidance and protection of angels in my life while in Colombia but none was as dramatic as experienced by my parents when they came to visit us when we lived in Cali. First let me give you a little background.

The first time my Dad saw my Mother she was going down Dead Man's Hill in Ensley, Alabama on a pair of skates. In amazement he remarked to a friend, "Look at that crazy girl!" Not long after that he married that "crazy girl" and lived a roller coaster ride with her for 44 years. In her youth, Mother was an all around athlete in high school, excelling in basketball and track. As long as I can remember a loving cup graced our mantle that was inscribed, "Kathryn Elizabeth Burnett, winner of the 100 yard dash, Ensley High School, March 1930." I can't remember how many times Mother said with a smile to Dad and me, "You may have a college education but neither of you have a loving cup."

Besides sports mother loved to travel to see new sights and search for exciting adventures. This may account for the classes in French she took in high school. Somewhere in the back of her mind she must have dreamed of traveling to France or another far-flung French port. Every time she had an opportunity to visit her son and family she did, sometimes with Dad and sometimes alone. It made no difference if I were in the east serving in the Army at South Carolina or the north while a pastor of a new church in Cleveland, Ohio or in Texas or Oklahoma on a church staff or in Costa Rica or Colombia serving as a missionary. Mother always found a way to visit us and we were always glad. Her last visit to Colombia was a real heart stopper and will confirm forever in my mind the presence of God's angels and their protective presence.

While teaching at the International Baptist Theological Seminary in Cali I was invited to attend a two-week religious education conference in Buenos Aires, Argentina beginning in January 1974. Marilyn thought it a great opportunity for her to accompany me in order to keep me out of trouble and make sure I made it there and back without any misadventures. The problem was, what do you do with four very active kids that were in school? Mother and Dad to the rescue. A quick call to Mother was all it took to get a commitment to stay with the kids while we were away in Argentina.

We were to leave Cali on New Year's Day so Mom and Dad had to travel during the Christmas season, the most congested time of the year for the flight. Our kids thought it was great timing because of all the Christmas gifts their grandparents would bring. We could hardly wait for their arrival.

On the day of their scheduled arrival the excitement mounted as we piled into the missionary van to make the 45 minute drive to the airport. Upon reaching the airport we all rushed to the waiting area overlooking the runways in order to get the best view of the planes and passengers as they arrived. We all watched with great anticipation as the Avianca plane from Bogota touched down at the Cali airport.

"Yes, Danny, Davy, Johnny, Jeannie; I believe the next ones to get off the plane will be your grandmother and grandfather!" That relieved their anxiety a little but when the last passenger deplaned and still no grandparents, we all began to worry. Could we have been mistaken about the date, time or flight number? I told Marilyn to wait in the car with the kids while I checked to see if there was any news about Mom and Dad.

After the attendant at the travel desk told me there were no other international flights coming into Cali that night I was approached by a woman who asked, "Would you happen to be Mr. Oliver?" When I said yes she told me this story: "I was sitting with your parents on the flight from Miami and when we landed at Bogota your mother said she needed to get off the plane to get a Coke for an aspirin." She took a deep breath and continued. "I went with your mother but the airport was very crowded and we were soon separated. After looking for her a few minutes I returned to the plane. Your dad asked if I would go back and have her paged but this didn't get any results either. Finally the flight attendant told your dad he should get off the plane and look for your mother because the plane had to go on to Cali. Your dad took all the hand luggage, got off the plane and we left for Cali. That was the last I saw of them."

By the time I got to the car and relayed the message to Marilyn and the kids I was in mild shock. Mother and Dad were somewhere in the city of Bogota, but where and in what condition? Bogota, the capitol of Colombia, has twice the population of the whole state of Alabama but that is not the worst part. The dangers of this South American capitol cannot be over-emphasized and especially for assumed rich foreigners that don't even speak the language. Like all cities of this size there are daily robberies, kidnappings and murders. It was midnight when we finally reached home and I immediately called fellow missionary Jimmy Stiles who lived in Bogota. Jimmy had come to Colombia after living near the Texas-Mexico border for many years and spoke Spanish like a native. Jimmy was also the adventurous type himself and if anyone could find my parents and would enjoy doing it, he could.

"Jimmy, sorry to call you so late," I began, "but I have a problem. My parents are lost somewhere in Bogota. Think you can find them?"

Briefly and to the point he said, "Well, I'll see what I can do and let you know as soon as something turns up." The situation was now in hand so after a prayer we all went to bed and went to sleep.

At two a.m. the phone rang. It was Jimmy. "Hey Jim, got some news for you. I've found your dad and he's here with me but haven't found your mom."

"Let me speak to Dad, Jimmy," I said.

"Sure, here he is."

"Dad, are you alright?" I asked.

"I"m a little tired but besides that I'm fine. Have you heard from your mother?"

"No Dad," I replied, "but I think it best for you to come on to Cali on the first flight tomorrow and if we haven't heard from Mother then I'll return to Bogota to look for her."

As I hung up the phone Marilyn and I looked at each in wild disbelief. We lay in the dark and talked about all the possibilities of what could have happened to mother and none of them were the least bit encouraging. If Mother and Dad had stayed together it would have been much safer for her but now she was alone somewhere in Colombia in the pitch dark of night. The thought of Mother as an unaccompanied woman who couldn't communicate in a large city at night sent the second wave of shock now over us. There would be no sleeping now!

About four o'clock in the morning we heard a car drive up and stop at our house. As the car door opened we heard a wonderful southern voice clearly say, "You can put the bags on the porch, here's ten dollars, good night and thank ya'll so much." It was mother! As we all rushed out to greet her amid the laughter and joy I almost shouted, "What in the world happened to you, Mother?"

Once safely inside she sat down, looking more pleased than exhausted, and related her incredible story. "When I was separated from my friend in the Bogota airport I didn't know how to get back to my plane so I began to follow some people getting on another plane. I gave my boarding pass to the flight attendant and sat down. When she asked where I was going I responded Cali. She said that plane wasn't going to Cali and pointed out the window to my plane nearby. As I got up, the Cali plane left so I sat back down. The flight attendant again said the plane I was on wasn't going to Cali. However, I told her that was where I was going so I stayed in my seat. We took off in a few minutes and after three stops we landed here in Cali. Two nice men and a woman from the airline were with me and when we passed the luggage department at the airport I saw our bags. They loaded them in a taxi and brought me here when I showed them your address." She paused, looked around and asked, "By the way, where is J.C?"

"Mother," I said, "Dad is in the capitol city of Bogota looking for you."

To my amazement Mother began laughing and said, "Isn't that funny, I beat J.C. to Cali."

It wasn't exactly funny to Dad when I called, telling him Mother had arrived safe and sound. His weak and very serious reply was, "Tell your mother I want a long talk with her when I get there tomorrow."

We only have a theory about Mother's trip but will probably never know the whole truth this side of heaven. I'm not real sure I want to know the whole truth. The trip to Cali from Bogota by jet takes about 45 minutes and is usually non-stop. During the day the plane occasionally has a stop-over in the city of Pereira but never at night because of the high Andes mountains in that area. Mother said the plane made three stops before arriving in Cali. The only possibility I know was that the plane flew north over a thousand miles and stopped at the costal towns of Barranquilla and Cartagena and then returned with Mother to Cali. If this wasn't enough, when she arrived in Cali she got her baggage with only a boarding pass.

A very tired J.C. Oliver arrived the next day followed by three Colombians carrying his hand luggage. He was so glad to see us and Mother that he forgot all about the conference he had planned the night before. After a good meal and a long siesta he told us his side of the story.

"When I got off the plane," he explained, "I was completely lost in the crowd and unable to talk to anyone. After I wandered around for a few minutes a man came up to me and asked in English if I had a problem. After I explained the situation to him he took me to the desk of the airline and said something to them in Spanish. He then told me to follow him to his car and after a short ride we arrived at a real nice hotel. He helped me register and told me he would be back the next day to take me back to the airport for the first flight to Cali. I tried to pay the man in dollars but he wouldn't take anything. I wasn't there long enough to go to sleep before Jimmy Stiles called and said he was coming to pick me up. I was very happy to see Brother Stiles. After a short night he took me to the airport where I caught the first flight to Cali."

How can one not believe in angels after an experience like this? I would like to add that after living about 30 years in Colombia I am persuaded that the angels were very likely aided by friendly Colombians. Everyone hears so much bad news about Colombia and naturally thinks everyone in this beautiful country is corrupt. This is far from the truth. In general, Colombians are very friendly and helpful and will go out of their way to assist you when in need. That's the real Colombia. I believe both Mom and Dad would agree heartily with me.

Mom and Dad stayed with the kids for two weeks while Marilyn and I made the trip to Argentina. I found out later that after the kids left for school Mom would slip out the door before Dad could lock it and head for town. She would catch the first bus that came along, ride it all over town looking at the people and the sights for an hour or two and then get off completely lost. She would flag a taxi, point at our home address written on a paper and pay him five dollars when she got home.

I asked her later, "Mom, what if the bus you got on wasn't going to town but going to another city as they often do? What would you have done?"

Her typical Kathryn Burnett Oliver response was, "I would have told them I live in Cali and please take me home." And do you know, I believe that would have happened.

We were very happy Mom and Dad could spend those

days with us and the children because that was the last time we ever saw her alive. That summer Mom and Dad attended a Gideon rally at the Alabama Baptist Assembly Camp where Mother played the piano. At the close of a very inspirational service Mother left the auditorium, suffered a heart attack and died there on those hallowed grounds.

I have often wondered how many angels the Lord has assigned to Mother in heaven. Possibly a legion. She'll need them all.

VII

ANSWERED PRAYER

Charles Spurgeon says this about prayer,

> The promise is part of the economy of our spiritual condition here below because it excites prayer. What is prayer but the promise pleaded? A promise is, so to speak, the raw material of prayer. Prayer irrigates the fields of life with the waters which are stored up in the reservoirs of promise. The promise is the power of prayer. We go to God, and we say to him, 'Do as thou hast said. O Lord, here in thy word; we beseech thee fulfil it.' Thus the promise is the bow with which we shoot arrows of supplication. It is a great thing to be driven to prayer by necessity; but it a far better thing to be drawn to it by expectation which the promise arouses.

It was during the years we served in Ohio that I was introduced to E.M. Bounds' book, *The Power of Prayer*. This little book on prayer and Spurgeon's sermons on promises have greatly influenced my life in the area of prayer. However, no book can ever come close to the Bible when it speaks on prayer. I could fill another book with all the scriptures and Biblical experiences related to the promises of prayer. I believe that Jesus' teaching in John 15 about the vine and the branches is the key to successful praying as well as fruit bearing. He said in John 15:7, "If ye abide in me and my words abide in you, ye shall ask what ye will, and it shall be done unto you." That is a powerful promise, but the condition must be met to receive the promise. As we abide in Christ through Bible study, prayer and service we grow in knowledge, wisdom and fruit bearing and can see more clearly what to ask for. We are therefore more successful in our praying. We no longer seek our will first but his, and our highest pleasure and joy is what brings praise and honor to him. As this becomes more and more a reality, our petitions are more in line with his will, and therefore granted. The Living Bible translates 1 Chronicles 17:25, 26 as, "Now I have the courage to pray to you, for you have revealed this to me. God himself has promised this good thing to me." Those revelations come from God as we abide in him and he in us.

While teaching in the Baptist Seminary in Cali I also served as pastor of a mission that had its worship services in the seminary chapel. We reached many middle class professionals who lived in the same community as the seminary. One young couple was very faithful to the Lord and was growing daily in their spiritual walk. They had one child and were expecting another, but after a few months of pregnancy she developed complications and was fearful of losing the baby. One day she called saying she had just returned from the obstetrician's office and was told that the baby was deformed and would never be a healthy child. The doctor feared for her life and advised her to abort the baby. She asked Marilyn and me to come to their home and pray for the Lord's guidance and strength to follow his will. When we arrived we found her in bed and distressed to the point of tears. We spoke to her about God's promises and his faithfulness to his children especially manifested in times of need such as this. We then knelt by the bed, took her hand and fervently prayed that his will would be revealed and that all involved would have the faith and courage to follow his way and not man's, whatever it meant. There was now a very noticeable change in our sister's attitude. As we left her home she said she felt God was leading her not to have an abortion, but to ask for a healthy and normal baby. That was the final decision of the couple and though she was confined to her bed during much of her pregnancy she delivered a healthy baby boy. The last time I saw him he was five years old and as active and healthy as any boy his age. Praise God for answered prayer to those who abide in him.

A beautiful promise of prayer in the Old Testament is 2 Chronicles 7:14. "If my people, which are called by my name, shall humble themselves and pray, and seek my face, and turn from their wicked ways; then will I hear from heaven and will forgive their sin, and will heal their land." Spiritual as well as physical blessings are promised for those who begin their return to God by humility and prayer.

Isaiah 65:24 says "And it shall come to pass, that before they call, I will answer; and while they are yet speaking I will hear."

The Psalmist says (91:15), "He shall call upon me and I will answer him, I will be with him in trouble; I will deliver him, and honour him."

The Apostle Paul was a great man of prayer who urges us to "pray without ceasing" and says in Romans 8:26 that the Holy Spirit will help us in praying properly. "Likewise the Spirit also helpeth our infirmities: for we know not what we should pray for as we ought: but the Spirit itself maketh intercession for us with groaning which cannot be uttered."

One of the most powerful promises of prayer is found in James 5:14-15, "Is any sick among you? Let him call for the elders of the church; and let them pray over him, anointing him with oil in the name of the Lord: and the prayer of faith shall save the sick, and the Lord shall raise him up; and if he have committed sins, they shall be forgiven him."

We were blessed in Colombia by many dedicated and well trained doctors. Dr. Eduardo DeLima, our personal physician in Cali, while on his way to work would stop by our home for house calls when needed. It was evident he took a personal interest in the health of Marilyn, me and all of our children. His father had sold the land to the seminary many years earlier when it wasn't popular to help the Baptists in any way.

One day we received a call from a fellow missionary asking us to go to the home of the DeLimas for an important reason that would be explained to us after we arrived. Upon arrival we were told by Dr. DeLima and his wife that a team of doctors had recently examined Dr. DeLima and found a very serious heart condition that required surgery. The operation could be done in Colombia but due to possible complications it was decided it would be best if they had the operation in the United States. However, they both had decided to ask their missionary friends to come to their home, place their hands on Dr. DeLima and pray for God's healing. It was very evident both had a strong faith in the healing power of God. Dr. DeLima moved to the center of the living room and knelt on the floor. We missionaries gathered around the beloved physician and placed our hands on his head and shoulders and after a slight pause we began to pray. Here were professors of the Old and New Testament, ethics, religious education, doctrine, evangelism as well as Baptist radio and television missionaries all joining together to ask God to heal one of his beloved children.

A few days later Dr. DeLima had to have another preliminary exam before taking the trip and there it was discovered his case wasn't as serious as previously diagnosed. The trip was postponed, and after several other examinations it was decided that Dr. DeLima would not have to have the operation at all and his medical colleagues pronounced him a well man. That has been over 20 years ago and as far as I know he never made that trip and never had the heart operation. The key to that story was the DeLimas, incentive to ask for the missionaries to pray for them, thus demonstrating the necessary faith in God to heal him.   God received the glory in this incident, no one claimed to have the gift of healing afterwards, and we all learned a lesson in prayer and faith.

A list of prayer promises would be incomplete without the following:

> Matthew 17:20 - faith as a mustard seed can remove mountains

> Matthew 7:7-11 - ask (shall receive), seek (and find), knock- (it shall be opened)

> Matthew 21:22 - all things received if asked in faith

> Matthew 18:19 - prayer answered if two agree on the request

This is only scratching the surface of promises related to prayer and maybe I have left out your favorite. To end this section of promises on prayer I will use 1 John 5:14-15. "And this is the confidence that we have in him, that if we ask anything according to his will, he heareth us. And if we know that he hear us, whatsoever we ask, we know that we have the petitions that we desired of him." This returns us to the first promise of answered prayer mentioned in this chapter; abiding in Christ and he in us for this prompts prayers within his will. These prayers are always answered.

Many times in our missionary career Marilyn and I sought God's guidance and help in prayer. As a young boy I was impressed by the missionary call and at a Royal Ambassador camp for boys I made my first decision to be a foreign missionary. That call became more definite to both Marilyn and me as we served, prayed and worked in Ohio. We left Ohio in the summer of 1964 to returned to the seminary, this time Southwestern in Ft. Worth, Texas. After one more year in the seminary and two years as pastor in Red Springs, Texas we were appointed to Colombia. Several times during our missionary career we were told the Colombian government wasn't giving visas to missionaries, but each time we went to the Lord in prayer. Each time he proved faithful to his promise and we were able to return and do the work he had called us to do. Prayer has been, is now and will always be a very important part of our life. Each morning Marilyn and I rise early, pray and read the Bible together and then have our private devotions apart. What a joy to live in Christ the Vine; communing with him daily and see him answer prayers.

VIII

HOLY SPIRIT POWER

Regarding the power of the Holy Spirit, Charles Spurgeon says:

> The Lord Jesus has not merely made us heirs of an infinite estate in the ages to come, but he has brought us into immediate enjoyment of a present portion; as saith the Scripture, 'In whom also we have obtained an inheritance.' The Holy Spirit is in many ways the means of making the promised heritage ours even now. By him we are 'sealed.' We know of a surety that the inheritance is ours, and that we ourselves belong to the great Heir of all things. Repentance, faith, spiritual life, holy desires, upward breathings, and even 'groaning which cannot be uttered,' are all proofs that the Holy Ghost is working upon us; and working in a way peculiar to the heirs of salvation.

Divinely inspired scripture as recorded by Joel 3:28,29

says, "And it shall come to pass afterward, that I will pour out my spirit upon all flesh; and your sons and your daughters shall prophesy, your old men shall dream dreams, your young men shall see visions: And also upon the servants and upon the handmaids in those days will I pour out my spirit." The church, on the day of Pentecost, received in full the promise of Joel and since then has been blessed throughout the centuries. These blessing have come to us, as members of his family, in many ways.

Acts 1:8 says, "But ye shall receive power, after that the Holy Ghost is come upon you; and ye shall be witnesses unto me both in Jerusalem, and in all Judea, and in Samaria and unto the uttermost part of the earth." The last earthly word of Jesus to his disciples was the divine commission to propagate the world with the gospel of salvation - and with that commission came the power to carry it out. When Marilyn and I went to Ohio and Colombia we were being obedient to that command as well as we knew how. Our strategy included three methods of work which we felt was given to us by the Holy Spirit. They were: beginning New Testament churches, training church members in personal soul winning and discipling the believers through a strong Sunday School program.

Jesus said to his disciples in John 4 that there are two classes of workmen in his vineyard - those that sow and those that reap. Sowing the gospel has been called pre-evangelism, teaching the Biblical truths about God so people can make knowledgeable decisions concerning his will for their lives. Reaping is evangelism - pulpit and personal. I have taken his words in John 4:38 as a very important part of my ministry, "I sent you to reap, that whereon ye bestowed no labor: other men labored and ye are entered into their labors." In no way do I minimize the work of sowing the gospel. That's a very important part of God's work. However, it seems to me there is a need for more reapers in the Lord's work. Reapers that receive the proper training and then go into the fields to lead the lost to Christ. This is the ministry, both in English and

Spanish, the Lord has led us to through the Holy Spirit. Marilyn and I have trained personal soul winners in the class room and on the job, in homes and in the streets. There has been a great multiplication, an explosion of trained soul winners in the past months and God is blessing churches and lives through this ministry. The future of this work for us, both in South America and the United States, is extremely exciting.

If it were left up to us alone to win lost people to Christ we would fail miserably, but God has given us his Spirit to do the hardest work. John 16: 8, 9 says the Holy Spirit is our helper in witnessing because he convicts the sinner of his lost condition. "And when he is come, he will reprove the world of sin and of righteousness and of judgement: of sin, because they believe not on me." I have seen children, young people and adults sit quietly and reflect on the gospel presented to them and respond in faith to Christ because the Holy Spirit had convicted them of their sins and need of a Savior.

A team of students and I visited a lawyer in Tierra Alta, Colombia during an evangelism clinic a few years ago. The gospel was clearly and powerfully presented to this young man and when given an opportunity to receive Christ into his heart and begin his eternal journey with the Lord he said, "My parents live with my wife and me and just this week we discussed the subject of God and his plan for our lives. We asked each other who could help us know the way and today you came and showed us the way." He graciously received Christ into his life during that visit. Who convicted this lawyer and his family? Who sent us to present the good news of salvation to him? The answer to both of these questions is the Holy Spirit.

I have been in many different types of religious services during my 50 years in the faith but there are none that can compare to those when soul winners return from the field with their testimonies of victory. I have stayed up until midnight listening to their reports and still wanted to hear more. Nothing in Christ's service, as far as I am concerned, can compare to the joys of seeing souls saved and soul winners trained. This joy is contagious! Stagnant and dead churches have come alive when laborers were trained and sent into the fields for the harvest. Psalm 92:14 says we can continue to bear fruit even in old age. Amen!

As in prayer the principle of the Vine and the branches is very important in bearing fruit. Jesus said in Matthew 4:19, "Follow me and I will make you fishers of men." In our daily walk with the Lord we receive instruction, inspiration and wisdom to be about the business of catching souls for God's kingdom. To be a fisher of men is a great honor and the Holy Spirit spoke clearly about this in Daniel 12:3, "And they that be wise shall shine as the brightness of the firmament; and they that turn many to righteousness as the stars for ever and ever."

We also have promises of success in this heavenly business. Psalm 126:5, 6 states a powerful promise: "They that sow in tears shall reap in joy. He that goeth forth and weepeth, bearing precious seed, shall doubtless come again with rejoicing, bringing his sheaves with him."

Galatians 6:9 teaches us we will have the victory but under one condition: "And let us not be weary in well doing: for in due season we shall reap, if we faint not." Plus our labor is not in vain. 1 Corinthians 16:58 says, "Therefore, my beloved brethren, be ye steadfast, unmovable, always abounding in the work of the Lord, forasmuch as ye know that your labor is not in vain in the Lord." Jesus summed it up by saying in Matthew 16:18, "And I say also unto thee, that thou art Peter, and upon this rock I will build my church; and the gates of hell shall not prevail against it." Satan is powerful but not as powerful as our Lord and his message.

No church should try to accomplish God's task by man's power nor should it hold back for a more convenient season. Expansion for God's soul winners is limitless. He says in Isaiah 54:2-3, "Enlarge the place of thy tent, and let them stretch forth the curtain of thine habitations: spare not, lengthen thy cords, and strengthen thy stakes; For thou shall break forth on the right hand and on the left; and thy seed shall inherit the Gentiles, and make the desolate cities to be inhabited." God promises to give us success in his work if we believe his word and launch out into the deep in the power of the Holy Spirit.

As Christians we have been baptized by the Holy Spirit at the new birth but we must continually ask for daily filling because we are still in the flesh and prone to grieve his Spirit. I have been in doctrinally sound churches that lack the Holy Spirit's power to accomplish God's work and they remind me of those Paul spoke of in 2 Timothy 3:5, "Having a form of godliness, but denying the power thereof."   I once heard someone say that ninety percent of the work of many churches today could be accomplished if the Holy Spirit was removed from its presence. That's sad if true even of one church.

Jesus said in Luke 11:13, "If ye then, being evil, know how to give good gifts unto your children: how much more shall your heavenly Father give the Holy Spirit to them that ask him?" If the task of a church is worldwide and we are willing to reap the lost and disciple the saved then we will need the power of God's Spirit to accomplish the task. Let us ask God to fulfill his promise, and let us believe his promises with all our heart, put our hands to the task and give our best in the work. Isaiah says to us "ye shall go out with joy." (55:12) God loves happy workers.

IX

HEAVENLY PROMISES

In Luke 10:20 Jesus said to the rejoicing seventy disciples that returned from their mission, "Notwithstanding in this rejoice not, that the spirits are subject unto you; but rather rejoice, because your names are written in heaven."

Spurgeon says:

> Jesus is the Fulfiller of the promise. His first Advent brought us the major part of the blessings which the Lord has foreordained for his own, and his second Advent is to bring us the rest. Our spiritual riches are linked with his ever-adorable person. Because he lives, we live; because he reigns, we reign; because he is accepted, we are accepted. Soon, at his manifestation, we shall be manifested; in his triumph, we shall triumph; in his glory, we shall be glorified. He is himself the Alpha and the Omega of the promises of God: in him we have life as sinners, in him we shall find glory as saints. If he be not risen, our hope is a

delusion; but since he has risen from the dead,
we are justified; since he will come in the glory
of the Father, we also shall be glorified.

The Living Bible translates the great truth of heaven in 1 Chronicles 17:17 like this: "For all the great things you have already done for me are nothing in comparison to what you have promised to do in the future."

Many "exceeding great and precious promises" are given to us as we pass through this earthly pilgrimage, but now we come to the last phase of God's riches, mainly the promises of our heavenly home and eternal fellowship with our God. We have been possessor of the Promis-Er (The one who makes the promises) from the first day we trusted Christ. Isaiah 7:14 and Matthew 1:23 both say, "they shall call his name Emmanuel, which being interpreted is, God with us." He has been present with us in Spirit on this earth but now we go to be with him in all glory. John described heaven as the Holy city, new Jerusalem, and said in Revelation 21:3, "Behold, the tabernacle of God is with men, and he will dwell with them, and they shall be his people, and God himself shall be with them, and be their God." What a heritage, what a future, what innumerable blessings await God's children! The apostle Paul had a glimpse of this future because he said in Philippians 1:21-23, "For to me to live is Christ, and to die is gain. But if I live in the flesh, this is the fruit of my labour: yet what I choose I want not. For I am in a strait betwixt two, having a desire to depart, and to be with Christ, which is far better." Let's take a closer look at "this far better" existence to help us have a clearer knowledge and evaluation of the riches prepared for us by God.

First, we must understand heaven is a real place. Jesus said in John 14:3, "I go to prepare a place for you." Jesus taught that God is the God of the living and these saints are not floating somewhere in outer space, but are together at home. That home is a place called heaven.

Second, heaven is a place prepared by the master architect

and builder. The same one who made the heavens and the earth and all within is also the master builder of heaven. Our world and universe defies description in beauty, complexity and scope, but heaven will be even better.

Third, the master architect and builder himself will be there. "Where I am, there ye may be also." While visiting a prospective church member one day I met a woman propagating her cultic beliefs who pointed her finger at me and asked, "Where will you be at the end of the world?" I answered, "That's the easiest question anyone has ever asked me in all my life." I then quoted this passage from John 14 and said I would be in heaven with Jesus. Then I asked her, "And where will you be? Jesus said, "No man cometh to the Father (Jehovah), but by me." She left without an answer.

Also, heaven is a prepared place for a prepared people. Negatively speaking it is not for the "cowardly, unbelieving, abominable liars." (Revelation 21:8) Positively, heaven is for those who have come through the spiritual birth by trusting in "the way, the truth and the life." The Bible repeats this promise of eternal life in heaven with God in many places but the best known references are found in the gospel of John, chapter 3. Abraham also received this promise and "looked for a city which hath foundations, whose builder and maker is God." (Hebrews 11:10) Promises of this city called heaven are described in many ways.

This inherited heaven is incorruptible. 1 Peter 1:3, 4 says, "Blessed be the God and Father of our Lord Jesus Christ which according to his abundant mercy hath begotten us again unto a lively hope by the resurrection of Jesus Christ from the dead, to an inheritance incorruptible, and undefiled, and that fadeth not away, reserved in heaven for you." Speaking of heaven John says in Revelation 21:27, "And there shall in no wise enter into it any thing that defileth." What a blessing it will be never to be tempted to sin again and to live in a society of sinless perfection.

Those who enter this city called heaven are greatly blessed

in every way. Revelation 22:14 says, "Blessed are they that do his commandments, that they may have right to the tree of life, and may enter in through the gates into the city."

Heaven is a place of pleasures and everlasting joys. Psalm 16:11, "Thou wilt show me the path of life: in thy presence is fullness of joy; at thy right hand there are pleasures for evermore." Paul says in 1 Corinthians 2:9, "Eye hath not seen, nor ear heard, neither have entered into the heart of man, the things which God hath prepared for them that love him."

Often promises of heaven are given in the negative. Revelation 21:4 says, "God shall wipe away all tears from their eyes; and there shall be no more death, neither sorrow, nor crying, neither shall there be any more pain: for the former things are passed away." Even though we have many promises to help us through this life we know our earthly pilgrimage, often spoken of in scripture as war, is plagued at times with tears, sorrow, pain and death.   But we Christians have a hope founded on the sure promise of God that one day these enemies will be no more. Thanks be to God!

There will be no sun or moon to give that great city light and warmth, for Revelation 21:23 promises, "And the city had no need of the sun, neither of the moon, to shine in it: for the glory of God did lighten it, and the Lamb of God is the light thereof." The whole earth would soon perish without the sun, but in heaven we shall have something - or better, someone - to give us physical and spiritual light, God himself. Revelation 22:5 adds that along with this light his children "shall reign for ever and ever."

There will be no need for a temple in heaven. Revelation 21:22, "And I saw no temple therein: for the Lord Almighty and the Lamb are the temple of it."   Verse 25 of this chapter says there is nothing to fear from without because, "the gates of it shall not be shut at all by day: for there shall be no night there."

There are many interpretations of the second coming of

Jesus but all of God's children are in agreement that Christ is coming again to claim his own and take them back with him to heaven. Jesus said in John 14:3, "I will come again, and receive you unto myself." When Christ ascended into heaven after his resurrection angels said unto his disciples, "Ye men of Galilee, why stand ye gazing up into heaven? this same Jesus, which is taken from you into heaven, shall so come in like manner as ye have seen him go into heaven." (Acts 1:11) There is great hope and comfort in this promise. Paul said to the Thessalonian Christians, "For the Lord himself shall descend from heaven ... comfort one another with these words." (1 Thessalonians 4:16, 18) The time of his second coming is unknown to us but the promise to all is that his appearance will be quick and unexpected. Matthew 24:42-44 gives the promise and warning, "Watch therefore: for ye know not what hour your Lord doth come. But know this, that if the good man of the house had known in what watch the thief would come, he would have watched, and would not have suffered his house to be broken up. Therefore be ye also ready: for in such an hour as ye think not the Son of man cometh." The next to the last verse in the Bible (Revelation 22:20) quotes Jesus as saying to us, "Surely I come quickly." And all of God's children say, "Come Lord Jesus."

Rewards in heaven may be something we don't understandl, but we must accept this truth since it is clearly taught in scripture. Psalm 58:11 says, "So that a man shall say, Verily there is a reward for the righteous: verily he is a God that judgeth in the earth." Paul builds on this truth in 2 Corinthians 5:10, "For we shall all appear before the judgement seat of Christ; that everyone may receive the things in his body, according that he hath done, whether it be good or bad." John, in Revelation 22:12, finishes this thought by quoting Jesus, "And behold, I come quickly; and my reward is with me, to give every man according as his work shall be." (See also Revelation 14:13)

One special reward is the crown that the faithful will

receive. Throughout scripture the Christian's promised crown is described in the following ways:

    Crown of glory - 1 Peter 5:3, 4
    Incorruptible crown - 1 Corinthians 9:25
    Crown of righteousness - 2 Timothy 4:8
    Crown of rejoicing - 1 Thessalonians 2:19
    Crown of life - James 1:12 and Revelation 2:10

Our promise is that "no man (shall) take thy crown," if we hold fast (Revelation 3:11) but the Lord shall be so worthy of our worship we will cast our crowns before his throne. (Revelation 4:11) Is there any wonder why, "blessed (happy) are the dead which die in the Lord," (Revelation 14:13) when we know we who have overcome in Christ shall sit with him on his throne? (Revelation 3:21)

I have purposely left the greatest promise of heaven, as I see it, until last. Two great men of God, David and John, had this revealed to them by the Spirit and passed it on to us in Holy writ. In Psalm 17:15 David said, "As for me, I will behold thy face in righteousness: I shall be satisfied, when I awake, with thy likeness." John gives us this promise in his first epistle, chapter 3, verse 2, "Behold, now are we the sons of God, and it doth not yet appear what we shall be: but we know that, when he shall appear, we shall be like him; for we shall see him as he is." I am disappointed and discouraged when I think about some of my thoughts and actions as well as my sins of omission. Is there no freedom from myself? God's promises say there is because someday I shall be changed into the likeness of my wonderful Savior and I say, "Thank you Lord for your unsearchable riches. Amen."

X

PROMISES THAT CANNOT BE LEFT OUT

Hebrews 4:1-3 give us the promise of entering into God's rest and the possibility of not claiming God's promise.

> Let us therefore fear, lest a promise being left us of entering into his rest, any of you should seem to come short. For unto us was the gospel preached, as well as unto them: but the word preached did not profit them, not being mixed with faith in them that heard it. For we which have believed do enter into rest, as he said, As I swore in my wrath, if they shall enter into my rest: although the works were finished from the foundation of the world."

Many of God's chosen people, the Hebrews that had been liberated from slavery in Egypt, were denied entrance into Canaan because of unbelief in the promise of God. There would be no rest in the promised land because the word preached to them was not mixed with faith. The writer of

Hebrews warns us that the same thing can happen to us and that we should fear missing what God has promised his children. Having these promises of God fulfilled in our lives is not automatic. There are things to learn - what the promises are; conditions to be met; prayers to plead the promises and faith in God to carry out what he has said he will do. The best description of this type of faith is found in God's word in Romans 1:17, Galatians 3:11 and Hebrews 10:38. The Christian is to live by faith. Hebrews says, "Now the just shall live by faith: but if any man draw back, my soul shall have no pleasure in him." Don't be disobedient as those Hebrew children were and miss what God has in store for you. It brings honor and glory to God's name when you claim that his word is true and you live in faith by its precepts. He is not pleased if you draw back in unbelief.

This book would be incomplete if certain promises were left out. Here are some promises that should be known and better still claimed by each Christian. Look them up in the Bible, believe them and God will bless you richly.

Assurance of eternal salvation - John 10:28, 29 and Romans 8:38, 39

God's loving kindness shall never depart from you - Isaiah 54:10

God displays his strength on our behalf - 2 Chronicles 16:9

All things are possible through faith - Mark 9:23

The Lord shall be my everlasting light - Isaiah 60:19, 20

Inner life renewed day by day - 2 Corinthians 4:16

God's word (promises) stands forever - Isaiah 40:8

Needs met for every good work - 2 Corinthians 9:8-11

God shall direct our way - Proverbs 3:5-6

He guides us with his voice - Isaiah 30:21

He guards our footsteps on the path - 1 Samuel 2:9

We can walk the path in confidence and not stumble - Proverbs 3:23

God's glory is my rear guard on the path - Isaiah 58:8

My path becomes brighter and brighter every day - Proverbs 4:18

Perfect peace - Isaiah 26:3

Renewed strength (eagle's wings) - Isaiah 40:31

Rejoice when I see Jerusalem - Isaiah 66:14

Though grief will come God will have compassion - Lamentations 3:32, 33

Strength when on bed of illness - Psalm 41:3

Help in times of trouble - Psalm 41:1

Joyful in God's house and our offerings will be accepted - Isaiah 56:6, 7

Spiritual growth - 2 Peter 1:8

Made a sharp cutting edge (evangelism) - Isaiah 41:15, 16

A fearless witness - Isaiah 44:8

Receive a hundred times more - Matthew 19:29; Mark 10:30; Luke 18:29, 30

A goodly inheritance (first, the Lord himself) - Psalm 16:5-7

Lend, but not borrow - Deuteronomy 28:12

Lack nothing good - Psalm 84:11

Given heart's desires - Psalm 37:4-5

Our righteousness shall shine as the light - Psalm 37:6

Safe in the Lord and fear no man - Proverbs 29:25

Scarlet sins become white as snow - Isaiah 1:18

Inherit the earth in peace - Psalm 37:11

Given wisdom, knowledge and joy - Ecclesiastes 2:26 - James 1:5

Fed with choicest foods - Psalm 81:16

Not fearful of hidden terrors - Psalm 91:5,6

Nothing can separate us from Christ's love - Romans 8:38,39

We are comforted by God and will comfort others - 2 Corinthians 1:4

Escape the corruption of the world - 2 Peter 1:4

Devil cannot touch us - 1 John 5:18

The devil flees from us - James 4:7

God works good in all things for us - Romans 8:28

Sweet sleep - Proverbs 3:24

Full of life and vitality in old age - Psalm 92:14

Our children mighty in the land - Psalm 112:2

Protected as an immigrant - Psalm 146:9

Receive the morning star - Revelation 2:28

Earth not destroyed again by water - Genesis 8:21,2

Make our feet as hinds feet - Habakkuk 3:19

Turn the hearts of the children to their fathers - Malachi 4:6

To the measure of my faith it shall be done - Matthew 9:29

Streams of living water flow through us - John 7:38

Even the casual reader of the Bible will recognize that I have presented only a small part of God's promises. You, dear reader, now have the opportunity to search out your own treasure. Let this be the beginning of your quest to know your riches in Christ Jesus and begin living by faith in his precious promises.

CONCLUSION

Charles Spurgeon sums it up when he says:

> If thou art a believer in the Lord Jesus, all the promises are thine; and among them is one for this very day of the month, and for this particular place wherein thou art now encamped: wherefore search the roll of thy Magna Carta, and find out thy portion for this hour. Of all the promises which the Lord hath given in his Book, he hath said, 'Not one of these shall fail, none shall want its mate, for my mouth hath commanded them.' Therefore trust, and be not afraid. Regardless of whatever else may prove to be a failure, the promise of God never will. Treasure laid up in this bank is beyond all hazard. "It is better to trust in the Lord than to put confidence in princes." (Psalm 118:9)

The opposite of putting our faith and hope in God's promises is to become disheartened, discourage, hopeless and despondent. The word "despond" is interesting because it comes from two Latin words: "de" -meaning down and "spondere" meaning promise. Therefore to despond and despair is to be down under or without a promise.

How many depressed Christians would be cured today if

they placed their faith in God's promises? Despondency and depression would turn to hope, joy and great expectations of the Lord. A promise points us to hope and success and inspires us to live our lives to the fullest.

May your motto be the same as Abraham's was when it was said of him in Romans 4:20-21, "He staggered not at the promise of God through unbelief; but was strong in faith, giving glory to God; And being fully persuaded that, what he had promised, he was able to perform."

According to Promise

By

C. H. Spurgeon

Contents

I.

A SIEVE NEEDED

It is very important to be able to distinguish between things that differ, for appearances are not to be relied upon. Things which seem to be alike may yet be the opposite of each other. A scorpion may be like an egg, and a stone like a piece of bread; but they are far from being the same. Like may be very unlike. Especially is this the case in spiritual things, and therefore it behoves us to be on our guard.

It would be very difficult to say how far a man may go in religion, and yet die in his sins; how much he may look like an heir of heaven, and yet be a child of wrath. Many unconverted men have a belief which is similar to faith, and yet it is not true faith. Certain persons exhibit pious affections which have the warmth of spiritual love, but are quite destitute of gracious life. Every grace can be counterfeited, even as jewels can be imitated, as paste gems are wonderfully like the real stones, so sham graces are marvelously like the work of the Spirit of God. In soul matters a man will need to have all his wits about him, or he will soon deceive his own heart. It is to be feared that many are already mistaken, and will never discover their delusion till they lift up their eyes in the world of woe, where their disappointment will be terrible indeed.

The dead child of nature may be carefully washed by its mother, but this will not make it the living child of grace. The life of God within the soul creates an infinite difference between the man who has it and the man who has it not; and the point is, to make sure that we have this life.

Are YOU sure that you have it?

It will be an awful thing to cry, "Peace, peace," where there is no peace, and to prophesy smooth things for yourself, and make your heart easy, and lull your conscience to slumber, and never to wake out of the sleep till a clap of the thunder of judgment shall startle you out of presumption into endless horror.

I desire to help my reader in the business of self-examination. I would have him go further than examination, and attain to such abundance of grace, that his holy and happy state shall become a witness to himself.

The first of this little book is meant to be a sieve to separate the chaff from the wheat. Let my friend use it upon himself; it may be the best day's work he has ever done. He who looked unto his accounts and found that his business was a losing one was saved from bankruptcy. This may happen also to my reader. Should he, however, discover that his heavenly trade is prospering, it will be a great comfort to him. No man can lose by honestly searching his own heart.

FRIEND, TRY IT AT ONCE.

II.

THE TWO SEEDS

"It is written, that Abraham had two sons, the one by a bondmaid, the other by a freewoman. But he who was of the bondwoman was born after the flesh; but he of the freewoman was by promise." Galatians 4:22,23

ABRAHAM had two sons. Ishmael and Isaac were beyond all dispute veritable sons of Abraham. Yet, one of them inherited the covenant blessing, and the other was simply a prosperous man of the world. *See how close these two were together!* They were born in the same society, called the same great patriarch "father," and sojourned in the same encampment with him. Yet, Ishmael was a stranger to the covenant, while Isaac was the heir of the promise. How little is there in blood and birth!

A more remarkable instance than this happened a little afterwards; for Esau and Jacob were born of the same mother, at the same birth, yet is it written, "Jacob have I loved, and Esau have I hated." One became gracious, and the other profane. So closely may two come together, and yet so widely may they be separated! Verily, it is not only that two shall be in one bed, and the one shall be taken, and the other left; but, two shall come into the world at the same moment, and yet one of them will take up his inheritance with God, and the other will for a morsel of meat sell his birthright. We may be in the same church, baptized in the same water, seated at the same communion table, singing the same psalm, and offering the same prayer; and yet we may be of two races as opposed as the seed of the woman and seed of the serpent.

Abraham's two sons are declared by Paul to be the types of two races of men, who are much alike, and yet widely differ. *They are unlike in their origin.* They were both sons of Abraham; but Ishmael, the child of Hagar, was the offspring of Abraham upon ordinary conditions: he was born after the flesh. Isaac, the son of Sarah, was not born by the strength of nature; for his mother was long past age. He was given to his parents by the Lord, and was born *according to the promise* through faith. This is a grave distinction, and it marks off the true child of God from him who is only so by profession. *The promise* lies at the bottom of the distinction, and the power which goes to accomplish the promise creates and maintains the difference. Hence *the promise,* which is our inheritance, is also our test and touchstone.

Let us use the test at once by seeing whether we have been wrought upon by the power which fulfills the promise. Let me ask a few questions, —How were you converted? Was it by yourself, by the persuasion of men, by carnal excitement; or was it by the operation of the Spirit of God? You profess to have been born again. Whence came that new birth? Did it come from God in consequence of his eternal purpose and promise, or did it come out of yourself? Was it your old nature trying to do better, and working itself up to its best form? If so, you are Ishmael. Or was it that you, being spiritually dead, and having no strength whatever to rise out of your lost estate, were visited by the Spirit of God, who put forth his divine energy, and caused life from heaven to enter into you? Then you are Isaac. All will depend upon the commencement of your spiritual life, and the source from which that life at first proceeded. If you began in the flesh, you have gone on in the flesh, and in the flesh you will die.

Have you never read, "That which is born of the flesh is flesh"? Before long the flesh will perish, and from it you will reap corruption. Only "that which is born of the Spirit is spirit"; the joy is that the spirit will live, and of it you will reap life everlasting. Whether you are a professor of religion or not, I beseech you, ask yourself—*Have I* felt the power of *the Spirit of God?*

Is the life that is within you the result of the fermentation of your own natural desires? Or is it a new element, infused, imparted, implanted from above? Is your spiritual life a heavenly creation. Have you been created anew in Christ Jesus? Have you been born again by divine power?

Ordinary religion is nature gilded over with a thin layer of what is thought to be grace. Sinners have polished themselves up, and brushed off the worst of the rust and the filth, and they think their old nature is as good as new. This toughing-up and repairing of the old man is all very well; but

it falls short of what is needed. You may wash the face and hands of Ishmael as much as you please, but you cannot make him into Isaac. You may improve nature, and the more you do so the better for certain temporary purposes; but you cannot raise it into grace. There is a distinction at the very fountain-head between the stream which rises in the bog of fallen humanity, and the river which proceeds from the throne of God.

Do not forget that our Lord himself said, "Ye *must be born again.*" If you have not been born again from above, all your church-going, or your chapel-going, stands for nothing. Your prayers and your tears, your Bible-readings and all that have come from yourself only, can only lead to yourself. Water will naturally rise as high as its source, but no higher: that which begins with human nature will rise to human nature; but to the divine nature it cannot reach. Was your new birth natural or supernatural? Was it of the will of man or of God? Much will depend upon your answer to that question.

Between the child of God and the mere professor there is a distinction as to origin of the most serious sort. Isaac was born *according to promise.* Ishmael was not of promise, but of the course of nature. Where nature's strength suffices there is no promise; but when human energy fails, the word of the Lord comes in. God had said that Abraham should have a son of Sarah; Abraham believed it, and rejoiced therein, and Isaac was born as the result of the divine promise, by the power of God. There could have been no Isaac if there had been no promise, and there can be no true believer apart from the promise of grace, and the grace of the promise.

Gentle reader, here let me inquire as to your salvation. Are you saved by what you have done? Is your religion the product of your own natural strength? Do you feel equal to all that salvation may require? Do you conclude yourself to be in a safe and happy condition because of your natural excellence and moral ability? Then you are after the manner of Ishmael, and to you the inheritance will not come; for it is not an inheritance according to the flesh, but according to promise.

If, on the other hand, you say, —*My hope lies only in the promise of God. He has set forth that promise in the person of his Son Jesus to every sinner that believeth in him; and I do believe in him, therefore I trust and believe that the Lord will fulfill his promise and bless me. I look for heavenly blessedness, not as the result of my own efforts, but as the gift of God's free favour. My hope is fixed alone upon the free and gratuitous love of God to guilty men, by the which he has given his son Jesus Christ to put away sin, and to bring in everlasting righteousness for those who deserve it not,"*—then this is another sort of language from that of the Ishmaelites, who say "We have

Abraham to our father." You have now learned to speak as Isaac speaks. The difference may seem small to the careless, but it is great indeed. Hagar, the slave-mother, is a very different person from Sarah, the princess. To the one there is no covenant promise, to the other the blessing belongs for evermore. Salvation by works is one thing; salvation by grace is another. Salvation by human strength is far removed from salvation by divine power; and salvation by our own resolve is the opposite of salvation by the promise of God.

Put yourself under this inquiry, and see to which family you belong. Are you of Ishmael or of Isaac?

If you find that you are like Isaac, born according to the promise, remember that your name is "Laughter"; for that is the interpretation of the Hebrew name Isaac. Take care that you rejoice with joy unspeakable and full of glory. Your new birth is a wonderful thing. If both Abraham and Sarah laughed at the thought of Isaac, you may certainly do so concerning yourself. There are times when, if I sit alone and think of the grace of God to me, the most undeserving of all his creatures, I am ready to laugh and cry at the same time for joy that ever the Lord should have looked in love and favour upon me. Yes, and every child of God must have felt the working of that Isaac nature within his soul, filling his mouth with Laughter, because the Lord hath done great things for him.

Mark well the difference between the two seeds, from their very beginning.

Ishmael comes of man, and by man. Isaac comes *by God's promise*. Ishmael is the child of Abraham's flesh. Isaac is Abraham's child, too; but then the power of God comes in, and from the weakness of his parents it is made clear that he is of the lord,—a gift according to promise. True faith is assuredly the act of the man who believes; true repentance is the act of the man who repents; yet both faith and repentance may with unquestionable correctness be described as the work of God, even as Isaac is the son of Abraham and Sarah, and yet he is still more the gift of God. The Lord our God, who bids us believe, also enables us to believe. All that we do acceptably the Lord worketh in us; yea, the very will to do it is of his working. No religion is worth a farthing which is not essentially the outflow of the man's own heart; and yet it must beyond question be the work of the Holy Ghost who dwells within him.

O friend, if what you have within you is natural, and only natural, it will not save you! The inward work must be supernatural; it must come of God, or it will miss the covenant blessing. A gracious life will be your own, even as Isaac was truly the child of Abraham; but still more it will be of God; for "Salvation is of the Lord." We must be born *from above*. Concerning all our religious feelings and actions, we must be able to say, "Lord, thou hast wrought all our works in us."

III.

THE TWO LIVES

"Neither, because they are the seed of Abraham, are they all children: but, In Isaac shall thy seed be called. This is, They which are the children of the promise are counted for the seed. For this is the word of promise, At this time will I come, and Sarah shall have a son." —Romans 9:7,8,9.

Ishmael and Isaac differed as to origin, and thence there was a difference *in their nature* which showed itself in their lives, and was chiefly seen in their relation to *the promise.*

According to the birth so will be the life which comes of it. In the case of the man who is only what he made himself to be, there will be only what nature gives him; but in the case of the man who is created anew by the Spirit of God, there will be signs following. "Of him are ye in Christ Jesus, who of God is made unto us wisdom, and righteousness, and sanctification, and redemption: as it is written, he that glorieth, let him glory in the Lord." There will be in the new-born man that which the new life brings with it: in the natural man there will be nothing of the kind.

Ishmael exhibited certain of the natural characteristics of Abraham joined with those of his slave mother. He was a princely man like his father, and inherited the patriarch's noble bearing; but Isaac had the faith of his father, and was in the succession as to holy inward spiritual life. As the heir of the promise, Isaac remains with his father Abraham, while Ishmael is forming camps of his own in the wilderness. Isaac seeks alliance with the olden stock in Mesopotamia; but Ishmael's mother takes him a wife out of Egypt, which was very natural, since she came from Egypt herself. Like will to like. Isaac meditated in the field at eventide, for his conversation was with sacred things; but Ishmael contended with all comers, for he minded earthly things. Meditation is not for the wild man, whose hand is against every man, and every man's hand against him. Isaac surrendered himself as a sacrifice to God; but you see nothing of that kind in Ishmael. Self-sacrifice is not for Ishmael; he is rather a killer and a slayer than a lamb that presents itself to God. So you shall find, that if you are religiously trained and tutored, and become "pious," as they call it, and yet are not renewed in heart, nor visited by the Holy Ghost, you will not live the secret life of the child of God. You may show many of the outward marks of a Christian; you may be able to sing, and to pray, and to quote Scripture, and perhaps to tell some little bits of imaginary experience; but you must be born again to know in very deed and truth the fellowship of the saints, communion in secret with the living God, and the yielding of yourself to him as your reasonable service. The child of the promise abides with God's people, and counts it his privilege to be numbered with them. The child of the promise feels that he is in the best company when no man can see or be seen, but when the Great Invisible draws near to him and holds converse with him. The child of the promise, and he only, is able to go up to the top of Moriah, there to be bound upon the altar, and to yield himself up to God. I mean by this last, that only he who is born of the Spirit will yield himself wholly to God, and love the Lord better than life itself. Your nature and conduct will be according to your origin; and therefore I pray that you may begin aright, so that as you profess to be a child of the kingdom, you may prove to be a true-born heir.

Ishmael, who was born after the flesh, the child of the bondwoman, must always bear the servile taint. The child of a slave is not free-born. Ishmael is not, cannot be, what Isaac is—the child of the free woman. Now mark: I do not say that Ishmael ever desired to be like Isaac; I do not say that he felt himself to be a loser by differing from Isaac; but, indeed, he was so. The man who is labouring for self-denials, may be proudly ignorant of his servile state; he may even boast that he was born free, and was never in bondage to any; and yet he spends his whole life in servitude. He never knows what liberty means, what content means, what delight in God means. He wonders when men talk about "full assurance of faith." He judges that they must be presumptuous. He has scarcely time to breathe between the cracks of the whip. He has done so much, but he must do so much more; he has suffered so much, but he must suffer so much more. He has never come into "the rest which remaineth for the people of God;" for his is born of the bondwoman, and his spirit is ever in bondage. On the other hand, he that is born of the free woman, and understands that salvation is of the grace of God from first to last, and that where God has given his grace he does not take it back, for "the gifts and calling of God are without repentance"—such a man accepting the finished work of Christ, and knowing his acceptance in the Beloved, rests in the lord, and rejoices exceedingly. His life and his spirit are filled with joy and peace, for he was born free, and he is free yea, free indeed.

Does my reader understand the freedom of the child of God? Or is he still in servitude under the law, afraid of being sent away into the wilderness? If you are in this latter case, you have not received *the promise,* or you would know that such a thing could not be. To Isaac, the child of *the promise,* the heritage belongs, and he abides forever, without fear of being cast out.

Those that are born as Ishmael was, according to the flesh, and whose religion is a matter of their own power and strength, mind earthly things, as Ishmael did. Only those that are born from above *through the promise* according to faith will, like Isaac, mind heavenly things. See how the naturally religious man minds earthly things. He is very regular at his place of worship; but while he is there he thinks of his business, his house, or his farm. Does he enjoy the worship of God? Not he! There is a sermon. Does he receive with meekness the engrafted word which is to save his soul? Not he! He criticizes it as if it were a political harangue. He gives his money to the cause of God as others do. Of course he does: for he feels that he has to quiet his conscience, and to keep up his good repute: but does he care for the glory of God? By no means. If he did he would give more than money. His heart's prayers would go up for the progress of the kingdom. Does he sigh and cry because of the sins of the times? Do you find him alone with God pouring out his heart in anguish because even in his own family there are those that are not converted to God? Did you ever see in him a high and holy joy when sinners are converted –an exultation because the kingdom of Christ is coming? Oh no, he never rises to that. All the service of God is outward to him: into the core and heart of spiritual things he has never entered, and he never can. The carnal mind, even when it is religious, is still enmity against God, and it is not reconciled to God, neither indeed can it be. There must be a spiritual mind created in the man, he must become a new creature in Christ Jesus, before he can appreciate, understand, and enjoy spiritual things.

To come back to where we started: "Ye must be born again." We must be born of the Spirit: we must receive a supernatural life by being quickened from our death in sin. We cannot bear the fruit of the spirit till we have the inner life of the Spirit. Ishmael will be Ishmael; and Isaac will be Isaac. As the man is, such will his conduct be. The man of sight, and reason, and human power, may do his best as Ishmael did; but only the child of the promise will rise to the life and walk of faith as Isaac did.

"*Hard lines,*" says one. Sometimes it is a great blessing to have those hard lines drawn, and drawn very straight, too. By this means we may be set on the right tract for eternity. One said the other day to a friend of mine, "I once went to hear Mr. Spurgeon, and when I went into the Tabernacle if you had asked me about myself I should have judged that I was as religious a man as ever lived in Newington, and as good a man, certainly, as ever made part of a congregation; but all this was reversed when I heard the gospel that day. I came out of the place with every feather plucked out of me. I felt myself the most wretched sinner that could be on the face of the earth, and I said I will never go to hear that man again, for he has spoiled me altogether." "Yes," he said, "but that was the best thing that could have happened to me. I was made to look away from myself, and all that I could do, to God and to his omnipotent grace, and to understand that I must pass under by Creator's hand again, or I could never see his face with joy." I hope my reader knows this truth for himself: a solemn truth it is. Even as first of all God made Adam, so must he make us over again, or else we can never bear his image, nor behold his glory. We must come under the influence of *the promise,* and live upon the promise, or our lives will never be guided by right principles, nor directed to right ends.

IV.

DIFFERING HOPES

"And as for Ishmael, I have heard thee: Behold, I have blessed him, and will make him fruitful and will multiply him exceedingly; twelve princes shall he beget, and I will make him a great nation. But my covenant will I establish with Isaac, which Sarah shall bear unto thee at this set time in the next year." –Genesis 17:20,21.

It is not at all wonderful that two persons, so different in their birth and nature as Ishmael and Isaac were, became very different in *their hopes*. To Isaac the covenant promise became the pole-star of his being; but for Ishmael no such light had risen. Ishmael aimed at large things, for he was the natural son of one of the greatest of men; but Isaac looked for still higher objects, because he was the child of the promise, and the inheritor of the covenant of grace which the Lord had made with Abraham.

Ishmael, with his high and daring spirit, looked to found a nation which should never be subdued, a race untamable as the wild ass of the desert; and his desire has been abundantly granted: the Bedaween Arabs are to this day true copies of their great ancestor. Ishmael in life and death realized the narrow, earthly hopes for which he looked; but on the roll of those who saw the day of Christ, and died in hope of the glory, his name is not entered. Isaac, on the other hand, saw far ahead, even to the day of Christ. He looked for a city which hath foundations, whose Builder and Maker is God.

Ishmael, like Passion, in "Pilgrim's Progress," had his best things here below: but Isaac, like Patience, waited for his best things for the future. His treasures were not in the tent and in the field, but in the "things not seen as yet." He had received the great covenant promise, and there he found greater riches than all the flocks of Nebaioth could minister to him. Upon his eye the day-star of promise had shone, and he expected a full moon of blessing in the fulness of the appointed time. The promise so operated upon him as to direct the current of his thoughts and expectations. Is it so with you, my reader? Have *you* received and embraced the promise of eternal like? You, therefore, hoping for things not seen as yet? Have you an eye to that which none can behold except believers in the faithfulness of God? Have you left the rut of present sensual perception for the way of faith in the unseen and eternal?

No doubt the reception of the promise, and the enjoyment of its hopes, influenced the mind and temper of Isaac, so that he was of a restful spirit. For him there were no wars and fightings. He yielded the present, and waited for the future. Isaac felt that as he was born after the promise it was for God to bless him, and to fulfill the promise that he had made concerning him; and so he remained with Abraham and kept himself aloof from the outside world. He both quietly hoped and patiently waited for the blessing of God. His eye was on the future, on the great nation yet to come, the promised land, and the yet more glorious promised seed in whom all the nations of the earth would be blessed. For all this he looked to God alone, wisely judging that he who gave.

the promise would himself see to its fulfillment. Because of this faith he was none the less active; yet he manifested none of the proud self-reliance which was so apparent in Ishmael. He was energetic in his own way, with a calm confidence in God, and a quiet submission to his supreme will. Year after year he held on in the separated life, and braved unarmed the danger which arose from his heathen neighbors—dangers which Ishmael confronted with his sword and with his bow. His trust was in that voice which said, "Touch not mine anointed, and do my prophets no harm." He was a man of peace, and yet he lived as securely as his warlike brother. His faith in the promise gave him hope of security, yea, gave him security itself, though the Canaanite was still in the land.

Thus does *the promise* operate upon our present life by creating in us an elevation of spirit, a life above visible surroundings, a calm and heavenly frame of mind. Isaac finds his bow and his spear in his God, Jehovah is his shield and his exceeding great reward. Without a foot of land to call his own, dwelling as a sojourner and a stranger in the land which God had given him by promise, Isaac was content to live upon the promise and count himself rich in joys to come. His remarkably quiet and equable spirit, while leading the strange unearthly life of one of the great pilgrim fathers, sprang out of his simple faith in the promise of the unchanging God. Hope, kindled by a divine promise, affects the entire life of a man in his inmost thoughts, ways and feelings: it may seem to be of less importance than correct moral deportment, but in truth it is of vital moment, not only in itself, but in that which it produces upon the mind, heart, and life. The secret hope of a man is a truer test of his condition before God than the acts of any one day, or even the public devotions of a year. Isaac pursues his quiet holy way till he grows old and blind, and gently falls asleep trusting in his God, who had revealed himself to him, and had called him to be his friend, and had said, "Sojourn in this land, and I will be with thee and bless thee, and in thy seed shall all nations of the earth be blessed."

As a man's hopes are, such is he. If his hope is in the promise of God, it is, it must be, well with him.

Reader, what are *your* hopes? "Why," says one, "I am waiting till a relative dies, and then I shall be rich. I have great expectations." Another hopes in his steadily growing trade; and a third expects much from a promising speculation. Hopes which can be realized in a dying world are mere mockeries. Hopes which have no outlook beyond the grave are dim windows for a soul to look through. Happy he who believes the promise, and feels assured of its fulfillment to himself in due time, and leaves all else in the hands of infinite wisdom and love. Such hope will endure trials, conquer temptations, and enjoy heaven below.

When Christ died on the cross our hopes began, when he rose they were confirmed, when he went up on high they began to be fulfilled, when he comes a second time they will be realized. In this world we shall have pilgrim's fare, and a table spread in the presence of our enemies; and in the world to come we shall possess the land which floweth with milk and honey, a land of peace and joy, where the sun shall no more go down, neither shall the moon withdraw herself. Till then we hope, and our hope layeth upon *the promise*.

V.

PERSECUTION CONSEQUENT ON THE PROMISE

"Now, we brethren, as Isaac was, are the children of promise. But as then he that was born after the flesh persecuted him that was born after the Spirit, even so it is now." Galatians 4:28,29.

When brothers differ so greatly as Ishmael and Isaac, it is not surprising if they fall out, and indulge unkind feelings. Ishmael was older than Isaac, and when the time came for Isaac to be weaned, his mother, Sarah, saw the son of the bond-woman mocking her child: so early had the difference of birth and condition begun to display itself. This may serve us as an indication of what we may expect if we possess the God-given life, and are heirs according to the promise. Those who are under the bondage of the law cannot love those who are free-born by the gospel, and in some way or other they soon display their enmity. We are not now thinking of the hostility between the wicked world and the church, but of that which exists between men of a merely natural religion, and those who are born of God. We speak not of the Philistines opposing Isaac, but of his brother Ishmael mocking him. Keenest of all is this opposition of the externally religious, to those who are born from above and worship God in spirit and in truth. Many precious children of God have suffered bitterly from the cruel hatred of those who professed to be their brethern.

Probably the motive of Ishmael was *envy;* he could not endure that the little one should have preeminence over himself. He seemed to say, "This is the heir, and therefore I hate him." Perhaps he mocked Isaac's *heir-ship,* and boasted that he had as good as the best of those who hope to be saved by the grace of God. They do not desire the grace of God themselves, and yet, like the dog in the manager, they cannot bear that others should have it: they envy the saints their hope, their peace of mind, and their enjoyment of the favour of God. If any of you find it so, be not in the least surprised.

The envy of Ishmael displaced itself most at the great feast which had been made at his brother's weaning; and even thus do formalists, like the elder brother in the parable, become most provoked when there is most occasion for rejoicing in connection with the Father's beloved child. The music and dancing of the true family are gall and wormwood to proud base-born professors. When full assurance is weaned from doubt, and holy delight is weaned from the world, then the carnal religionist puts on a sneer, and calls the godly mad, or fanatical, or murmurs with sullen sarcasm, "Poor fools! Let them alone; they are a sadly deluded crew." People who are religious but not truly regenerated, who are working and hoping to be saved by their own merits, usually exhibit a bitter hatred towards those who are born of the promise.

Sometimes they mock their *feebleness.* May be Ishmael called Isaac a mere baby, just weaned. So are believers a feeble folk, and exceedingly likely to excite the derision of those who think themselves strong-minded. Isaac could not deny that he was weak, neither can believers deny that they are faulty, and are subject to infirmities which may put them under just censure: but the world makes more of this than justice will allow, and mocks at saints for weaknesses which in others would be overlooked. We must not think it a strange thing if our insignificance and imperfection should set proud and self-righteous Pharisees jerring at us and our Gospel.

Frequently the sport is raised by the believer's *pretensions*. Isaac was called "the heir," and Ishmael could not bear to hear it. "Look," says the legalist, "yonder man was not long ago a known sinner; now he says he has believed in Jesus Christ, and therefore he declares that he knows himself to be saved and accepted, and sure of heaven. Did you ever hear of such presumption?" He who hugs his chains hates the presence of a free man. He who refuses the mercy of God because he proudly trusts his own merits, is angry with the man who rejoices to be saved by grace.

Perhaps the little Isaac, the child of such aged parents, seemed *odd and strange* to the young half-bred Egyptian. No person is so much a foreigner to his fellow-men as a man born from above. To live by faith upon the promise of God ought to seem the most proper and natural thing in the world; but it is not so esteemed: on the contrary, men count those to be strange beings who believe in God, and act upon such a belief. Wretched boys in the streets still hoot at foreigners, and men of the world still jest at true believers, because of their unworldly spirit and conduct. To us this is a testimony for good, for our Lord said, "If ye were of the world, the world would love his own; but because ye are not of the world, but I have chosen you out of the world, therefore the world hateth you."

In a thousand ways, many of them so petty as to be unworthy of mention, the believer can be made to bear "trials of cruel mockings," and he ought to be prepared so to do. After all, it is but a small matter to be persecuted nowadays; for the fires of Smithfield are quenched, the Lollards' tower contains no prisoners, and not even a thumb-screw remains in use. Courage, good brother! Even should you be ridiculed, no bones will be broken; and if you are brave enough to despise contempt, even your sleep will not be disturbed.

Ismael's mocking Isaac is only one among ten thousand proofs of the enmity which exists between the seed of the woman and the seed of the serpent. The mixture of these two in Abraham's household came about through his going down into Egypt and acting in an unbelieving manner towards Pharaoh. Then the Egyptian bondwoman was given to Sarah, and the evil element came into the camp. Sarah, in an evil hour, gave the bondwoman to her husband; hence ten thousand tears. No association of the unregenerate with the Church of God will avail to alter their nature: an Ishmael in Abraham's encampment is Ishmael still. Today, the fiercest enemies of the truth of God are the aliens in our communion. These are they who make believers in sound evangelical teaching look like strangers in the Churches which were founded on the basis of scriptural doctrine. They make us foreigners in our own land. They are lenient to all manner of heresy; but the believer in the doctrines of grace they sneer at as old-fashioned and bigoted—a belated mortal who ought studiously to seek out a grave and bury himself. Yet will the man who trusts his God and believes in his covenant, be able to survive all mockeries; for he counts the reproach of Christ greater riches than all the treasures of Egypt. It is by no means shameful to trust God: on the contrary it is a point of honour with good men to trust in Him who is faithful and true; and if they have to suffer for it they do so joyfully. Gird yourselves, therefore, with a holy courage, you who learning through grace to live upon *the promise* of God by faith. Was not the great Head of the family despised and rejected of men? Must not the rest of the brotherhood be conformed to the first-born? If we are made partakers of Christ's sufferings, we shall be partakers of his glory; wherefore, let us take part and lot with the Crucified heir of all things.

VI.

THE PARTING

"Nevertheless what saith the scripture? Cast out the bondwoman and her son; for the son of the bondwoman shall not be heir with the son of the freewoman." —Galatians 4:30

Isaac and Ishmael lived together for a time. The self-religionist and the believer in the promise may be members of the same church for years, but they are not agreed, and cannot be happy together, for their principles are essentially opposed. As the believer grows in grace and enters upon his spiritual manhood, he will be more and more disagreeable to the legalist, and it will ultimately be seen that the two have no fellowship with one another. They must separate, and this is the word that will be fulfilled to the Ishmaelite: "Cast out this bondwoman and her son: for the son of this bondwoman shall not be heir with my son, even with Isaac." Grievous as the parting may be, it will be according to the divine will, and according to the necessities of the case. Oil and water will not mingle, neither will the natural man's religion agree with that which is born of *the promise*, and sustained by the promise.

Their parting will be only the outward result of a serious difference which always existed.

Ishmael was sent away, but he soon ceased to regret it; for he found greater freedom with the wild tribes of the country, among whom he soon became a great man. He prospered much, and became the father of princes. He was in his proper sphere in the wide world; there he had honour and gained a name among its great ones. Often it happens that the carnally religious man has many excellent habits and ways about him; and having a desire to shine, he goes into society, and is appreciated and becomes notable. The world is sure to love its own. The aspiring religionist usually forsakes his first friends, and openly declares, "I have given up the old-fashioned style of religion. The saints were all very well while I was poor, but now I have made a fortune I feel that I must mix with a more fashionable set of people." He does so, and has his reward. Ishmael had his portion in this life, and never expressed a desire to share in the heavenly covenant and its mysterious blessings. If my reader would feel freer and more at home in society than in the church of God, let him know assuredly that he belongs to the world, and let him not deceive himself. As his heart is, such is he. No measure of force-work can turn Ishmael into Isaac, or a worldling into an heir of heaven.

Outwardly, and in this present life, the heir of the promise did not appear to have the best of it. Nor, indeed, should this be expected, since they who choose their heritage in the future have, in fact, agreed to accept trial in the present.

Isaac experienced certain afflictions which Ishmael never knew: he was mocked, and he was at last laid on the altar; but nothing of the sort happened to Ishmael. You, who like Isaac are the children of the promise, must not envy those who are the heirs of this present life, though their lot seems easier than your own. Your temptation is to do so; even as the Psalmist did when he was grieved because of the prosperity of the wicked. There is in this fretting a measure of running back from our spiritual choice: have we not agreed to take our part of the future rather than in the present? Do we rue the bargain? Moreover, how absurd it is to envy those who are themselves so much to be pitied! To lose the promise is practically to lose everything; and the self-righteous have lost it. These worldly professors have no spiritual light or life, and they desire none. What a loss, to be in the dark and not to know it! They have enough religion to make them respectable among men, and comfortable in their own consciences; but this is a sorry gain if they are abominable in the sight of God. They feel no inward fightings and wrestlings; they find no contention of the old man against the new; and so they go through life with a jaunty air, knowing nothing till their end come. What wretchedness to be so besotted! Again, I say, do not envy them. Better far is the life of Isaac with its sacrifice, than that of Ishmael with its sovereignty and wild freedom; for all the worldling's greatness will soon be ended and leave nothing behind it but that which will make the eternal world to be the more miserable.

Yet dream not that believers are unhappy. If in this life only we had hope we should be miserable indeed; but *the promise* lights up our whole career, and makes us truly blessed. God's smile beheld by faith gives us fullness of joy. Put the believer's life at the greatest possible disadvantage, paint it in the darkest colours, take away from it not only comforts but necessaries, and even then the Christian at his worst is better than the worldling at his best. Let Ishmael have the whole world; ay, give him as many worlds as there are stars in the midnight sky, and we will not envy him. It is ours still to take up our cross, and to be strangers and foreigners with God in this land, as all our fathers were; for the promise, though it seems far off to others, we do, by faith, realize, and embrace, and in it we find a heaven below. Abiding with God, and with his people, we count our lot far better than that of the greatest and most honoured of the children of this world. The prospect of our Lord's second coming, and of our own eternal glory in fellowship with him, suffices to fill us with content while we wait for his appearing.

This difference on earth will lead to a sad division in death. The child of the bondwoman must be cast out in eternity as well as in time. None can enter heaven who claim it by their own doings, or boast that they have won it on their own strength. Glory is reserved for those who are saved by grace, and none who trust in self can enter there. What a terrible thing it will be when those who laboured to establish their own righteousness, and would not submit to the right-eousness of Christ, shall be driven out! How ill they then envy those lowly ones who were fain to accept pardon through the blood of Jesus! How will they discover their folly and wicked-ness in having despised the gift of God by preferring their own righteousness to that of the Son of God!

As the persons who are represented by Ishmael and Isaac are ultimately parted, so the principles upon which they rest must never be mingled, for they can by no means be made to agree. We cannot be saved in part by self, and in part by the promise of God. The principle and notion of earning salvation must be expelled from the mind. Every degree and form of it must be "cast out." If we are so unwise as to place our dependence partly on grace and partly on merit, we shall be resting one foot on a rock and the other on the sea, and our fall will be certain. There can be no dividing of the work or of the glory of salvation. It must be all of grace or all of works, all of God or all of man; but it cannot be half of one and half of the other. Cease from the vain attempt to unite two principles which are as adverse as fire and water. *The promise,* and the promise alone, must be the foundation of our hope, and all legal notions must be sternly dismissed as irreconcilable with salvation by grace. We must not begin in the spirit, and hope to be made perfect in the flesh. Our religion must be all of a piece. To sow with mingled seed, or to wear a garment of linen and woolen mixed, was forbidden to the Lord's ancient people; and to us it is unlawful to mingle mercy and merit, grace and debt. Whenever the notion of salvation by merit, or feeling, or ceremonies comes in, we must cast it out without delay, though it be as dear to us as Ishmael was to Abraham. Faith is not sight; the spirit is not the flesh; grace is not merit; and we must never forget the distinction, lest we fall into grievous error and miss the heritage which belongs only to the heirs according to promise.

Here is our confession of faith:—

"Knowing that a man is not justified by the works of the law, but by the faith of Jesus Christ, even we have believed in Jesus Christ, that we might be justified by the faith of Christ, and not by the works of the law: for the works of the law shall no flesh be justified."—Galatians 2:16

Here also is the clear line of distinction as to the method of our salvation, and we desire to keep it plain and manifest:—

"Even so then at this present time also there is a remnant according to the election of grace. And if by grace, then it is no more of works: otherwise grace is no more grace. But if it be of works, then it is no more grace: otherwise work is no more work." —Romans 11:5,6

Reader, do you see this?

VII.

WHOSE ARE THE PROMISES?

THE LORD is ever just and good towards his creatures: it is his nature so to be. But there was no necessity either in his justice or in his goodness that he should make promises of grace to those who had rebelled against him. Man has forfeited every form of claim upon his Maker, which he may have thought he had; for he has broken the pure and holy law which he was under bond to have obeyed. Nothing is now due to man but the reward of sins. If God should now deal with man upon the ground of strict justice he must condemn and punish him. Anything in the way of favour to a guilty creature must proceed only from the undeserved mercy and sovereign goodness of God: it must spring spontaneously from the goodwill and pleasure of the Most High. *The promises* of grace flow from the boundless love of God, and from that alone. They could not have proceeded from any other source. No single one of the race of man has any natural right to promises of blessing, nor can the whole world of men deserve them. God has made promises to men of his own free will and good pleasure, from no motive but that which lies within himself.

He has chosen to make his promises to elect persons, who in process of time are discovered by their exercising faith in him. Those whom God has chosen are led by the Holy Spirit to choose God and his way of salvation by faith in Christ Jesus. Those of the elect that come to years of discretion are led to faith in Jesus; and all who have faith in him may conclude beyond doubt that they are of the chosen number to whom the promises are given. To those who live and die in unbelief there is no absolute and personal promise of God: they are not under grace but under law, and to them belong the threatenings and not the promises. These prefer another method of dealing to that of gracious promise, and in the end they perish as the result of their foolish preference. The chosen of the Lord are led to relinquish the proud way of self and merit: they take to the road of faith, and so find rest unto their souls. To believe the word of God, and to trust in him whom God has sent to be our Savior may seem a small thing; but indeed it is not so: it is the sign of election, the token of regeneration, the mark of coming glory. So to believe that God is true as to rest one's eternal interests upon his promise, bespeaks a heart reconciled to God, a spirit in which the germ of perfect holiness is present.

When we believe God as he is revealed in Christ Jesus, we believe all *his promises*. Confidence in the Person involves confidence in all that he speaks: hence we accept all the promises of God as being sure and certain. We do not trust one promise and doubt another, but we rely upon each one as true, and we believe it to be true to *us* so far as it has respect to our condition and circumstances. We argue from general statements to particular applications, He who has said that he will save those who believe in him will save *me* since I believe in him; and every blessing which he has engaged to bestow upon believers he will bestow upon *me* as a believer. This is sound reasoning, and by it we justify the faith by which we live and are comforted. Not because I deserve anything, but because God has freely promised it to me in Christ Jesus, therefore I shall receive it: this is the reason and ground of our hope.

One wonders at first sight that all men do not believe God. It would seem as if this mark of divine election would be universally present; for God cannot lie, and there is no reason to suspect him of change, or failure of ability to keep his word. Yet, so false is the heart of man, that man doubts his Maker. He hates his God, and therefore disbelieves him. It is the surest proof of man's natural enmity against God that he dares to impute falsehood to one who is truth itself. "He that believeth not God hath made him a liar; because he believeth not the record that God gave of his Son" (I John 5:10).

Real, practical trust in the living God, easy as it seems to be, is a virtue which was never practised by an unrenewed heart. The glorious atonement made by the incarnate Son of God is worthy of the reliance of all mankind. One would have imagined that every sinner would have washed at once in this cleansing fountain, and without hesitation would have believed in the divine Redeemer: but it is very far from being so. Men will not come unto Christ that they may have life. They would rather trust in anything than in the sacrifice of Jesus. Until the Holy Ghost works a miracle upon a man, he will not confide in the great sacrifice which God has provided and accepted for the putting away of guilt. Hence it is that this simple, commonplace matter of faith, yet becomes the distinguishing mark of the chosen of the Lord. No other token is so infallible: "He that believeth on him hath everlasting life." Feelings and actions may all serve as evidences; but the master evidence of an interest in the promise of God is faith in him. "Abraham believed God, and it was counted to him for righteousness": there were many other good points in the patriarch's character, but this was the decisive one, —he believed God; indeed, this was the root of all else that was commendable in him.

Worldly-wise men despise faith, and set it in contrast with virtuous actions; but this contrast is not fair: one might as well contrast a fountain with its stream, or the sun with its own heat. If true faith be the mother of holiness, let the mother grace have praise because of its offspring, and let it not be contrasted therewith. Such unfair reasoning comes of wanton malice: if men loved good works as much as they pretend to do, they would love the faith which produces them.

God loves faith because it honours him, and also because it leads to acts of obedience to him, which obedience includes love to our fellow-men. There is more in faith than meets the eye. It is in one aspect the greatest of all good works, even as our Lord Jesus teaches us. The Jews said to him (John 6:28,29) "What shall we do, that we might work the works of God?" They would fain perform God-like works, works above all others approved of the Lord. Jesus answered them, "This is the work of God, that ye believe on him whom he hath sent." As much as to say—the most divinely approved work possible to you, is to believe in the Messiah. To trust in the Lord Jesus is the climax of virtue. Proud men may sneer, but this statement is true. "Without faith it is impossible to please God;" but "he that believeth in him is not condemned." *The promise* is made to him that believes the promise, and to him it shall be fulfilled. He who embraces the promise is embraced by the promise. He who accepts Christ is accepted in Christ. He who truly believes is surely saved.

READER, DO YOU BELIEVE YOUR GOD?

VIII.

THE PROMISE A FREE GIFT

"Whereby are given unto us exceeding great and precious promises." —II Peter 1:4

OBSERVE that word *"given."* Peter says, "Whereby *are given* unto us exceeding great and precious promises." We are beholden for everything to the gift of God. We live upon divine charity. All that we have received as a gift, and all we are to have must come in the same way. "The wages of sin is death, but the gift of God is eternal life." We are unable to earn anything, but God is able to give all things. Salvation must be all a gift, a spontaneous gift of divine love. *The promise* of salvation is of the same nature.

"It is more blessed to give than to receive"; and he that is most blest of all, the ever-blessed God, delights to give. It is as much his nature to give as it is the nature of the sun to shine, or of a river to flow. How blessed we are in being receivers! This is emphasized greatly, when we reflect how necessary it is that we should receive; for the things that we need are such that if we do not obtain them we are lost now, and lost for ever. We are without life, without light, without hope, and without peace, if we are without God. If God does not give to us according to the riches of his grace, we are then worse than naked, and poor, and miserable; we are utterly and altogether undone, It is not possible that we should deserve such rich gifts. Even if we could deserve anything, these must come to us without money and without price. A promise from God must be a boon of grace: we cannot claim that God should promise us his favour, and the priceless boons which are wrapped up in it.

This teaches us what posture to take up. Pride ill becomes dependents. He who lives upon gifts should be humble and grateful. We are beggars at the door of mercy. At the beautiful gate of the temple we sit down every day to ask an alms, not of the worshippers, but of him whom angels worship. As often as our Lord passes by, we ask and he gives; nor are we surprised that we received from his love; for he has promised to bestow great mercies. He taught us to say, "Give us this day our daily bread," and therefore we are neither ashamed nor afraid to ask all things from him. Ours is a life of dependence, and we delight to have it so. It is sweet to take all things from the hands of our crucified Lord. Happy is the poverty which leads us to be rich in Christ. We earn nothing, and yet receive everything, thrice blest in being hourly partakers of the gift of God. "Whereby are *given* unto us exceeding great and precious promises."

Beloved, this teaching as to *the promise* coming of pure gift should be exceedingly encouraging to all who feel their lost estate, and own that they are spiritually bankrupt. To such it is a word of good cheer, that everything is freely *given* to us of God: who should he not give to them as well as to other needy ones? Those of us who rejoice in God have received all things as a free gift: why should not others receive the like: They say, "There is nothing freer than a gift": why should not my reader receive as well as myself? To one who is willing to give, poverty, on the part of the receiver, is a recommendation instead of an obstacle. Come, then, you who are without merit, Christ will be your merit. Come, you that have no righteousness, he will be your righteousness. Come, you who are as full of sin as an egg is full of meat, and the pardoning Lord will put away your sin. Come, you who are utterly forlorn and be made rich in Jesus. The trade of a mendicant will suit you, and you will prosper in it: for I see you have a cruel hunger, and an empty wallet. He that cannot dig should not be ashamed to beg. A begger needs no stock-in-trade. "Old shoes and clouted," rags worn and foul—these form a fit livery for a beggar. Are you not dressed in this fashion spiritually? The poorer the wretch, the more welcome is he at the door of divine charity. The less you have of your own, the more welcome you are to him who giveth freely and upbraideth not.

> "Come, ye needy, come and welcome,
>
> God's free bounty glorify;
>
> True belief, and true repentance,
>
> Every grace that brings us nigh,
>
> Without money,
>
> Come to Jesus Christ and buy."

Yes, it is all a gift. This is the gospel that we are sent to preach to you—"God so loved the world

That he gave his only begotten Son, that whosoever believeth in him should not perish, but have everlasting life. This is the record, that God hath given to us eternal life, and this life is in his Son"(I John 5:11). On God's part it is all giving; on our part it is all receiving. *The promise* is already made, and freely made: it will be fulfilled, and freely fulfilled. God does not begin with giving, and then go on to charging a price. No commission is payable upon receipt of his grace. He does not ask or receive a farthing; his love is altogether a gift. As a gift you may accept his promise: he will not degrade himself by listening to any other terms.

The word given in the text is a plain invitation to the poorest of the poor. Oh that they would make bold to avail themselves of it! The great bell is ringing, ringing that all who will to come to the great table of infinite liberality may hear it and draw near. Freely, according to the riches of his grace, doth God promise salvation and eternal life to all who believe on his Son, Jesus Christ. His promise is firm and sure, why is it that men do not believe it?

Reader, what say you to the promise so freely given to all believers? Will you believe it and live thereby?

IX.

THE PROMISE OF GOD
A REALITY.

SURELY it is a wonderful thing that the eternal God should make promises to his own creatures. Before he pledged his word he was free to do as it pleased him: but after he has made a promise, his truth and honour bind him to do as he has said. To him indeed, this is no limiting of his liberty; for the promise is always the declaration of his sovereign will and good pleasure, and it is ever his delight to act according to his word: yet is it marvelous condescension for the free spirit of the Lord to form for itself covenant bonds. Yet he hath done so. The Lord has made a covenant of grace with men, in which he has confirmed his promises, not only by pledging his word, but by giving his oath: "that by two immutable things in which it was impossible for God to lie, we might have strong consolation who have fled for refuge to lay hold upon the hope set before us."

In that covenant there are promises many and precious, all confirmed in Christ Jesus, and established for ever upon the foundation of divine truthfulness. This is our hope, even as Paul wrote to Titus: "In hope of eternal life, which God, that cannot lie, promised before the world began." God has promised of our faithful Creator. To help us so to trust, the promises were not only spoken but written. Men say they like to have an agreement in black and white, and we have it so in this case. "In the volume of the book it is written." In the page of inspiration the record stands: and as we believe our Bibles, we are bound to rely upon the promises contained therein.

It is a cause of much weakness to many that they do not treat *the promises* of God as realities. If a friend makes them a promise, they regard it as a substantial thing, and look for that which it secures: but the declarations of God are often viewed as so many words which mean very little. This is most dishonouring to the Lord, and very injurious to ourselves. Rest assured that the Lord never tribles with words: "Hath he said, and will he not do it?" His engagements are always kept. David said of the Lord's promises to him, "Yet hast thou made with me an everlasting covenant, ordered in all things and sure." God speaks deliberately, in due order and determination, and we may depend upon it that his words are sure, and will be fulfilled as certainly as they are uttered. Have any who have trusted in the Lord been confounded? Can instance be found in which our God has been false to his word? The ages cannot produce a single proof that the promise-making Jehovah has run back from that which he has spoken.

We admire fidelity in men, and we cannot imagine it to be absent from the character of God, and therefore we may safely reckon upon his being as good as his word. It is said of Blucher, that when he was marching to help Wellington at Waterloo, his troops faltered. "It can't be done," said they. "It *must* be done," was his answer. "I have promised to be there—*promised*, do you hear? You would not have me break my word." He was at Waterloo to good purpose: he would not be hindered, for his promise was given. We praise such faithfulness; we should think little of one who did not exhibit it. Shall the Lord God Almighty fail in his promise? No, he will move heaven and earth, and shake the universe, rather than be behind-hand with his word. He seems to say –"It *must* be done. I have promised –promised do you hear?" Sooner than his promise should fail, he spared not his own Son. Better Jesus die than the word of the Lord be broken. I say again, —depend upon it, the Lord means what he says, and will make good every syllable. Yet none but the chosen seed will believe him, *Reader,* will you?

God must be true, whoever else may deceive. If all the truth in the whole world could be gathered together, it would be but as a drop in the bucket compared with the truthfulness of God. The veracity of the most just of men is vanity itself compared with the sure truth of God. The faithfulness of the most upright of men is as a vapour, but the faithfulness of God is as a rock. If we trust in good men we ought infinitely more to trust in the good God. Why does it seem a singular thing to rest on the promise of God? Somehow it looks to many to be a dreamy, sentimental, mystical business; and yet if we view it calmly it is the most matter of fact transaction that can be. God is real: all else is shadowy. He is certain: all else is questionable. He must keep his word, this is an absolute necessity: how else could he be God? To believe God should be an act of the mind which needs no effort. Even if difficulties could be suggested, the simple and pure in heart should spontaneously say "Let God be true and every man a liar." To give God less than an implicit faith is to rob him of an honour justly due to his spotless holiness.

Our duty to God demands that we accept his promise, and act upon it. Every honest man has a right to credence, and much more does the God of truth deserve it. We ought to treat the promise as in itself the substance of the thing promised, just as we look upon a man's cheque or note of hand as an actual payment. Promises to pay are passed from hand to hand in daily business, as if they were current money of the merchant; and God's promises should be regarded in the same light. Let us believe that we have the petitions which we have asked of him. He warrants our so doing, and promises to reward such faith.

Let us regard the promise as a thing so sure and certain that we act upon it, and make it to be a chief figure in all our calculations. The Lord promises eternal life to those who believe in Jesus; therefore, if we really believe in Jesus, let us conclude that we have eternal life, and rejoice in the great privilege. The promise of God is our best ground of assurance; it is far more sure than dreams and visions, and fancied revelations; and it is far more to be trusted than feelings, either of joy or sorrow. It is written, "He that believeth in him is not condemned." I believe in Jesus, therefore I am not condemned. This is good reasoning, and the conclusion is certain. If God has said so, it is so, beyond all doubt. Nothing can be more certain than that which is declared by

God himself; nothing more sure to happen, than that which he has guaranteed by his own hand and seal.

When a soul is under conviction, it perceives *the threatenings* of the Lord with an intensity of belief which is very noticeable, since its awe-stricken faith breeds within the heart overwhelming terror and dismay. Why should not *the promise* be accepted with a similar realization? Why not accepted with the same certainty? If it be made true in the conscience that he that believeth not shall be damned, it may be accepted with equal assurance, that he that believeth and is baptized shall be saved, since the latter is as much the word of God as the former. The tendency of the awakened mind, is to dwell upon the dark side of God's word, and feel the full force of it; and at the same time to neglect the brighter portion of the record, and cast a doubt upon it, as though it were too good to be true. This is folly. Every blessing is too good for us to receive if we measure it by our unworthiness; but no blessing is too good for God to give, if we judge of it by his surpassing excellence. It is after the nature of a God of love to give boundless blessing. If Alexander gave like a king, shall not Jehovah give like a God?

We have sometimes heard persons say, "As sure as death"; we suggest that we might as fitly say, "As sure as life," Gracious things are as sure as "terrible things in righteousness. Whosoever believeth in Jesus shall not perish, but have everlasting life." It must be so, for God's word hath said it, and there can be no mistake about it.

Yes, the Lord means what he says. He never mocks men with barren words and empty sounds. Why should he deceive his creatures, and ask from them a barren confidence? The Lord may go beyond his work in giving more than it might be thought to mean; but he can never fall short of it. We may interpret his promises upon the most liberal scale. He never falls below the largest rendering which expectation can give to the promise. Faith never yet outstripped the bounty of the Lord. Let us embrace the promise, and rejoice that it is substance and not shadow. Let us even now rejoice in it as being the reality of that for which we are hoping.

X.

THE PECULIAR TREASURE OF BELIEVERS

GOD's promises the treasure of believers: the substance of faith's heritage lies in them. All the promises of our covenant God are ours to have and to hold as our personal possession. By faith we receive and embrace them, and they constitute our true riches. We have certain most precious things in actual enjoyment at this present; but the capital of our wealth, the bulk of our estate lies in *the promise* of our God. That which we have in hand is only the earnest penny of the immeasurable wage of grace which is to be paid to us in due time.

The Lord graciously gives us even now all things necessary for this life and godliness; but his choicest blessings are held in reserve for time to come. Grace given to us from day to day is our spending money for traveling expenses on the road home; but it is not our estate. Providential supplies are rations on the march, but not the ultimate feast of love. We may miss these wayside meals, but we are bound for the Supper of The Lamb. Thieves may rob us of our ready cash;

but our peculiar treasure is hid with Christ in God beyond all fear of loss. The Lamb which bled to make this treasure ours is keeping it for us.

It is a great joy to have a full assurance of our interest in the promises: but this joyful feeling we may lose, and we may find it hard to get it again, and yet the eternal inheritance will be quite as truly ours. It is as though a man should have in his hand a fair copy of his title-deeds, and should much delight himself in reading it until by some mischance his copy is stolen or mislaid. The loss of his writings is not the loss of his rights. His comfortable reading of the title-deed is suspended, but his claim to his property is not shaken. The covenant promise is entailed upon every joint-heir with Christ, and there is no such thing as the breaking of this entail. Many an event may tend to shake the believer's sense of security, but "the promise is sure to all the seed." Our greatest possession lies not in any present comfort or confidence which we receive from the promise, but in *the promise* itself, and in the glorious heritage which it secures to us. Our inheritance lies not on this side Jordon. Our city of habitation is not within the borders of the present: we see it from afar, but we wait for its full enjoyment in that illustrious day when our covenant Head shall be revealed in his glory, and all his people with him. God's providence is our earthly pension; but God's *promise* is our heavenly heritage.

Did it ever occur to you to enquire why the way of God's dealing with his chosen should be by promise? He could have bestowed his blessings at once, and without giving us notice of his intention. In this way he would have obviated the necessity of a covenant concerning them. There was no necessity in the nature of things for this plan of promising. The Lord might have given us all the mercies we needed, without pledging himself to do so. God, with his great strength of will, and firmness of purpose, could have secretly resolved in himself to do all that he does unto believers without having made them the confidants of his divine counsels. Many a decree hath he kept secret from the foundations of the world; why, then, hath he revealed his purposes of blessing? Why is it that his dealings with his people from the gate of Eden till now have been upon the footing of publicly expressed promises?

Does not the question answer itself? In the first place, *we could not have been believers if there had not been a promise in which to believe.* If the system of salvation is to be by faith, a promise must be made upon which faith can exercise itself. The plan of salvation by faith is selected because it is most suitable to the principle of grace; and this involves the giving of promises, that faith may have both food and foundation. Faith without a promise would be a foot without ground to stand upon; and such a faith, if faith it could be called would be unworthy of the plan of grace. Faith being chosen as the great evangelical command, the promise becomes an essential part of the gospel dispensation.

Moreover, it is a charming thought that *our good God designedly gives us promises of good things that we may enjoy them twice: first by faith, and then by fruition.* He gives twice by giving by promise; and we also receive twice in embracing the promise by faith. The time for the fulfillment of many a promise is not by-and-by; but by faith we realize the promise, and the foreshadowing of the expected blessing fills our souls with the benefit long before it actually comes. We have an instance of this upon a large scale in Old Testament saints. The great promise of the seed in whom the nations should be blessed was the ground of faith, the foundation of hope, and the cause of salvation to thousands of believers before the Son of God actually appeared among men. Did not our Lord say "Abraham saw my day: he saw it, and was glad"? The great father of the faithful saw the day of Christ through the telescope of God's promise, by the eye of faith; and though Abraham did not obtain the fulfillment of that promise, but fell asleep before the coming of the Lord, as did Isaac, and Jacob, and many others of the saints, yet he had Christ to trust in, Christ to rejoice in, and Christ to love and serve. Before he was born in Bethlehem, or offered upon Calvary, Jesus was so seen of the faithful as to make them glad. The promise gave them a Savior before the Savior actually appeared. So it is with us at this time: by means of the promise we enter into possession of things not seen as yet. By anticipation we make the coming blessing present to us. Faith obliterates time, annihilates distance, and brings future things at once into its possession. The Lord has not as yet given us to join the hallelujahs of heaven; we have not yet passed through the gates of pearl, nor have we trodden the streets of transparent gold; but the promise of such felicity lights up the gloom of our affliction, and yields us immediate foretastes of glory. We triumph by faith before our hands actually grasp the palm. We reign with Christ by faith before our heads are incircled with our unfading coronets. Many and many a time we have seen the dawn of heaven while we have beheld light breaking from the promise. When faith has been vigorous we have climbed where Moses stood and gazed upon the land which floweth with milk and honey; and then, when Atheist has declared that there is no Celestial City, we have answered, "Did we not see it from the Delectable Mountains?" We have seen enough by means of the promise to make us quite sure of the glory which the Lord hath prepared for them that love him; and thus we have obtained our first draught of the promised bliss, and found therein a sure pledge of our full and final enjoyment of it.

Do you not think that the promise also is intended *to lead us constantly away from the things that are seen, onward and upward to the spiritual and the unseen?* The man who lives on the promise of God has risen into quite another atmosphere than that which oppresses us in these low lying vales of daily life. "It is better, says one, to trust in the Lord than to put confidence in men. It is better to trust in the Lord than to put confidence in princes." And so, indeed, it is; for it is more spiritual, more noble, more inspiring. We need to be raised to this elevated trust by divine power; for our soul naturally cleaveth unto the dust. Alas! We are hampered by our idolatrous desire to see, and touch, and handle: we trust our senses, but have not sense enough to trust our God. The same spirit which led Israel to cry in the Wilderness, "Make us gods to go before us," leads us to sigh for something tangible by flesh and blood, whereon our confidence may take hold. We hunger for proofs, tokens, and evidences, and will not accept the divine promise as better and surer than all visible signs. Thus we pine away in hungering for tokens and evidences which are visible, till we are driven to try the better and surer things which are invisible. Oh, it is a blessed thing for a child of God to be made to quit the sand of things temporal for the rock of things eternal, by being called upon to walk by the rule of the promise!

Furthermore, *the promises are to our hearts a help to the realization of the Lord himself.* The child of God, when he believes the promise, is brought to feel that God is, and that he is the rewarder of them that diligently seek him. Our tendency is to get away from a real God. We live and move in the region of materialism, and we are apt to be enthralled by its influences. We feel these bodies to be real when we have pain in them, and this world to be real when we are weighed with its crosses: yet the body is a poor tent, and the world a mere bubble. These visible things are unsubstantial, but they appear sadly solid to us: what we need is to know the invisible to be quite as real as that which is seen, and even more so. We need a living God in this dying world, and we must have him truly near us, or we shall fail. The lord is training his people to perceive himself: the promise is part of this educational process.

When the Lord gives us faith, and we rest on his promise, then are we brought face to face with him. We ask, "Who gave this promise? Who is to fulfill this promise? And our thoughts are thus led into the presence of the glorious Jehovah. We feel how necessary he is to the whole system of our spiritual life; and how truly he enters into it, so that in him we live, and move, and have our being. If the promise cheers us, it is only because there is God at the back of it; for the more words of the promise are nothing to us except as they come from the lips of God who cannot lie, and except as they are wrought out by that hand which cannot fail. The promise is the forecast of the divine purpose, the shadow of the coming blessing; in fact, it is the token of God's own nearness to us. We are cast upon God for the fulfillment of his engagements, and that is one of his reasons for dealing with us after the method of promise. Perhaps if the Lord had dropped our mercies at our door without a previous hint of their coming, we should not have cared to know whence they came. If he had sent them with unbroken regularity, even as he makes his sun to rise every morning, we might have slighted them as common results of natural laws, and so have forgotten God because of the punctuality of his providence. Certainly we should have lacked that grand test of the being and loving-kindness of God which we now receive as we read the promise, accept it by faith, plead it in prayer, and in due season see it fulfilled.

That regularity of divine bounty which ought to sustain and increase faith is often the means of weakening it. He whose bread comes to him by a government annuity or a quarterly rent, is tempted to forget that God has any hand in it. It ought not to be so; but through the hardness of our hearts such an ill result does frequently follow from the constancy of a gracious providence.

I should not wonder if those Israelites who were born in the wilderness, and had gathered manna every morning for years, had also ceased to wonder at it, or to see the hand of the Lord in it. It ought not to be so; but through the hardness of our hearts such an ill result does frequently follow from the constancy of a gracious providence.

I should not wonder if those Israelites who were born in the wilderness, and had gathered manna every morning for years, had also ceased to wonder at it, or to see the hand of the Lord in it. Shameful stupidity! But, ah, how common! Many a person has lived from hand to mouth, and seen the hand of the Lord in the gift of every morsel of bread: at last by God's goodness he has prospered in this world, and obtained a regular income, which he has received without care and trouble, and shortly he has come to look at it as the natural result of his own industry, and has no longer praised the loving-kindness of the Lord. To be living without the conscious presence of the Lord is a horrible state of affairs. Supplied, but not by God! Sustained without the hand of God! It were better to be poor, or sick, or exiled, and thus to be driven to approach our heavenly Father. To avoid our coming under the curse of forgetting God, the Lord is pleased to put his choicest blessings into connection with his own promises, and to call forth our faith in reference to them. He will not allow his mercies to become veils to hide his face from the eyes of our love; but he makes them windows through which he looks upon us. The Promiser is seen in the promise, and we watch to see his hand in the performance; thus are we saved from that natural atheism which lurks within the heart of man.

I think it well to repeat that *we are put under the regime of promise in order that we may grow in faith.* How could there be faith without a promise? How growing faith without grasping more and more of the promise? We are made to remember in the hour of need, that God has said, "Call upon me in the day of trouble, and I will deliver thee." Faith believes this word, calls upon God, and finds herself delivered thus she is strengthened, and made to glorify the Lord.

Sometimes faith does not find the promise fulfilled at the moment; but she has to wait a while. This is fine exercise for her, and serves to test her sincerity and force; this test brings assurance to the believer, and fills him with comfort. By-and-by the answer is given to prayer, the promised boon is bestowed, faith is crowned with victory, and glory is given to God; but meanwhile the delay has produced the patience of hope, and made every mercy to wear a double value. Promises afford training - ground for faith: these are poles and leaping-bars for the athletic exercise of our young faith, by the use of which it grows to be so strong that it can break through a troop, or leap over a wall. When our confidence in God is firm we laugh at impossibility, and cry, "It shall be done"; but this could not be if there were not an infallible promise wherewith faith could gird itself.

Those promises which as yet are unfulfilled are precious helps to our advance in the spiritual life. We are encouraged by exceeding great and precious promises to aspire to higher things. The prospect of good things to come strengthens us to endure, and to press forward. You and I are like little children who are learning to walk, and are induced to take step after step by an apple being held out to them. We are persuaded to try the trembling legs of our faith by the sight of a promise. Thus we are drawn to go a step nearer to our God. The little one is very apt to cling to a chair, it is hard to get it to quit all hold, and venture upon its feet; but at last it becomes daring enough for a tiny trip, which it ends at its mother's knees. This little venture leads to another and another, till it runs alone. The apple plays a great part in the training of the babe, and so does the promise in the education of faith. Promise after promise have we received, till now, I trust, we can give up crawling on the earth, and clinging to the things which rest upon it, and can commit ourselves to the walk of faith.

The promise is a needful instrument in the education of our souls in all manner of spiritual graces and actions. How often have I said, "My Lord, I have received much from thee, blessed be thy name for it; but there is yet a promise more which I have not enjoyed; therefore I will go forward till I attain its fulfilment! The future is an unknown country, but I enter it with thy promise, and expect to find in it the same goodness and mercy which have followed me hither to; yea, I look for greater things than these."

Nor must I forget to remind you, that the promise is part

of the economy of our spiritual condition here below because it excites prayer. What is prayer but the promise pleaded? A promise is, so to speak, the raw material of prayer. Prayer irrigates the fields of life with the waters which are stored up in the reservoirs of promise. The promise is the power of prayer. We go to God, and we say to him, "Do as thou hast said. O Lord, here is thy word; we beseech thee fulfill it." Thus the promise is the bow by which we shoot the arrows of supplication. I like in my time of trouble to find a promise which exactly fits my need, and then to put my finger on it, and say, "Lord, this is thy word; I beseech thee to prove that it is so, by carrying it out in my case. I believe that this is thine own writing; and I pray thee make it good to my faith." I believe in plenary inspiration, and I humbly look to the Lord for a plenary fulfillment of every sentence that he has put on record. I delight to hold the Lord to the very words that he has used, and to expect him to do as he has said, because he has said it. It is a great thing to be driven to prayer by necessity; but it is a better thing to be drawn to it by the expectation which the promise arouses. Should we pray at all if God did not find us an occasion for praying, and then encourage us with gracious promises of an answer? As it is, in the order of providence we are tried, and then we try the promises; we are brought to spiritual hunger, and then we are fed on the word which proceedeth out of the mouth of God. By the system which the Lord follows with his chosen we are kept in constant intercourse with him, and are not allowed to forget our heavenly Father: we are often at the throne of grace, blessing God for promises fulfilled, and pleading promises on which we rely. We pay innumerable visits to the divine dwelling-place, because there is a promise to plead, and a God waiting to be gracious. Is not this an order of things for which to be grateful? Ought we not to magnify the Lord that he doth not pour upon us showers of unpromised blessings, but he enhances the value of his benefits by making them the subjects of his promises and the objects of our faith?

XI.

THE VALUATION OF THE PROMISES

"Whereby are given unto us exceeding great and precious promises." —II Peter 1:4

We have thought upon *the promises* as our treasure: it is time that we should take a survey of them, and calculate their value. Since the promises are our estate, let us form a correct estimate of our wealth: possibly we may not fully know how rich we are. It will be a pity to pine in poverty from ignorance of our large property. May the Holy Spirit help us to form a due valuation of the riches of grace and glory reserved for us in the covenant of promise!

The apostle Peter speaks of the promises as *"exceeding great and precious."* They do indeed exceed all things with which they can be compared. None ever promised even to the half of their kingdoms; but what of that? God promised to give his own Son, and even his own Self, to his people; and he did it. Princes draw a line somewhere, but the Lord sets no bounds to the gifts which he ordains for his chosen.

The promises of God not only exceed all precedent, but they also exceed all imitation. Even with God himself for an example, none have been able to vie with him in the language of liberality. The promises of Jehovah are as much above all other promises as the heavens are above the earth.

They also exceed all expectation. He does for us "exceeding abundantly above all that we ask or even think." Nobody could have imagined that the Lord would have made such promises as he has made: they surpass the dreams of romance. Even the most sanguine hopes are left far behind, and the loftiest conceptions are outdone. The Bible must be true, for it could not have been invented: the promises contained in it are greater for quantity and better for quality than the most expectant could have looked for. God surprises us with the surpassing fullness of his cheering words: he overwhelms us with favours till, like David, we sit down in wonder, and cry, "Whence is this to me?"

The promises exceed all measurement: there is an abyss of depth in them as to meaning, a heaven of height in them as to excellence, and an ocean of breath in them as to duration. We might say of every promise, "It is high: I cannot attain to it." As a whole, the promises exhibit the fullness and all-sufficiency of God: like God himself they fill all things. Unbounded in their range, they are everywhere about us, whether we wake or sleep, go forth or return. They cover the whole of life from the cradle to the tomb. A sort of omnipresence may be ascribed to them: for they surround us in all places, and at all times. They are our pillow when we fall asleep, and when we awake they are still with us. "How precious also are thy thoughts unto me, O God! How great is the sum of them!" "Exceeding" all conception and calculation; we admire them and adore their Giver, but we can never measure them.

The promises even exceed all experience. Those men of God who have known the Lord for fifty or sixty years have never yet extracted the whole of the morrow from his promise.

Still it might be said, "the arrow is beyond thee." Somewhat better and deeper yet remains to be searched out in the future. He who dives deepest be experience into the depths of the divine promises is fully aware that there is yet a lower depth of grace and love unfathomable. The promise is longer than life, broader than sin, deeper than the grave, and higher than the clouds. He that is most acquainted with the golden book of promise is still a new beginner in its study: even the ancients of Israel find that this volume passeth knowledge.

Certainly I need not say that the promises exceed all expression. If all the tongues of men and of angels were given me, I could not tell you how great are the promises of God. They exceed not only one language, but all languages: they surpass the glowing praises of all the enthusiasts that have ever spoken. Even angels before the throne still desire to look into these marvels, for they cannot yet reach the mystery –the length, and breadth, and height. In Christ Jesus everything exceeds description; and the promises in him exhaust the force of all speech, human or divine. Vain is it for me to attempt the impossible.

Exceeding *"great"* Peter says they are; and he knew right well. They come from a great God, they assure us of great love, they come to great sinners, they work for us great results, and deal with great matters. They are as great as greatness itself; they bring us the great God, to be our God for ever and ever. God's first promise was that in which he engaged to give us his Son. We are wont to say, "Thanks be unto God for his unspeakable gift," but let not the words glide too easily over the tongue. For God to give his Only-begotten Son is beyond all conception a great deed of love: indeed, "great" seems too little a word to describe such a miracle of love. When the Lord had given his Son, freely delivering him up for us all—what then? He promised to give the Holy Ghost, the Comforter, to abide with us for ever. Can we measure the value of that great promise? The Holy Ghost came down at Pentecost, in fulfil-ment of that ancient prophecy: was not that marvelous descent an exceeding great and precious gift? Remember that the Holy Spirit works in us all those graces which prepare us for the society of heaven. Glory be to God for this visitation of boundless grace!

What next? Our Lord has given us now the promise that he will "come again a second time without a sin offering unto salvation." Can all the saints put together fully measure the greatness of the promise of the Second Advent? This means infinite felicity for saints. What else has he promised? Why, that because he lives we shall live also. We shall possess an immortality of bliss for our souls; we shall enjoy also a resurrection for our bodies; we shall reign with Christ; we shall be glorified at his right hand. Promises fulfilled and promises unfulfilled, promises for time and promises for eternity—they are indeed so great that it is impossible to conceive of their being greater.

"What more can he say than to you he hath said?

You who unto Jesus for refuge have fled."

O ye whose minds are trained to lofty thought, tell me your estimate of the faithful promises! I perceive a promise of the pardon of sin. O ye forgiven ones, declare the greatness of this boon! There is the promise of adoption. Children of God, you begin to know what manner of love the Father hath bestowed on you in this; tell out your joy! There is the promise of help in every time of need. Tired ones, you know how the lord sustains and delivers his chosen; proclaim the largeness of his grace! There is the promise that as your day your strength shall be. You that are working hard for Christ, or bearing his cross from day to day, you feel how exceeding great is that promise of sure support. What a word is this: "All things work together for good to them that love God, to them who are the called according to his purpose"! Who can estimate the breadth of such a gracious assurance? No, you need not take that foot-rule from your pocket: it will not serve you here. If you could take the distance of a fixed star as your base, all reckoning would still be impossible. All the chains that ever measured the acres of the wealthy are useless here. A certain millionaire glories that his estate reaches from sea to sea; but no ocean can bound the possessions secured to us by the promise of our faithful God. The theme is so exceeding great that it exceeds my power of expression, and therefore I forbear.

The verse, upon which we are now thinking, speaks of "exceeding great *and precious promises.*" Greatness and preciousness seldom go together; but in this instance they are united in an exceeding degree. When the Lord opens his mouth to make a promise, it is sure to be worthy of him: he speaks words of exceeding power and richness. Instead of trying to speak of the preciousness of the promises doctrinally, I will fall back upon the experience of those who have tried and proved them.

Beloved, how precious the promises are to the poor and needy! They that know their spiritual poverty discern the value of the promise which meets their case. How precious, also, are the promises, to those who have enjoyed the fulfillment of them! We can go back in memory to times and seasons when we were brought low, and the Lord helped us according to his word. Even before he brought us up out of the horrible pit, we were kept from sinking in the deep mire by looking forward to the time when he would appear for our rescue. His promise kept us from dying of hunger long before we reached the feast of love. In the expectation of future trial our confidence is in the promise. Thus it is very precious to us even before it is actually fulfilled. The more we believe the promise, the more we find in it to believe. So precious is the word of the Lord to us, that we could part with everything we have rather than throw away a single sentence of it. We cannot tell which promise of the Lord we may next need: that which we have hardly noticed may yet turn out at a certain moment to be essential to our life. Thank God, we are not called to part with any one of the jewels from the breastplate of Holy

Scripture: they are all yea and amen in Christ Jesus to the glory of God by us!

How precious are the promises when we lie sick, gazing into eternity by the month together, sorely tried and tempted through pain and weariness! All depressing circumstances lose their power for evil when our faith takes firm hold upon the promises of God. How sweet to feel I have my head on the promise, and my heart on the promise: I rest on the truth of the Most High! Not on earthly vanity, but on heavenly verity, do I repose. There is nothing to be found elsewhere comparable to this perfect rest. The pearl of peace is found among the precious promises. That is precious indeed which can support dying men, and cause them to pass into eternity with as much delight as if they were going to a marriage-feast. That which lasts forever, and lasts good forever, is most precious. That which brings all things with it, and hath all things in it, —that is precious indeed; and such is the promise of God.

If such be the greatness and preciousness of the promises, *let us joyfully accept and believe them.* Shall I urge the child of God to do this? No, I will not so dishonour him; surely he will believe his own Father! Surely, surely, it ought to be the easiest thing in the world for the sons and daughters of the Most High to believe in him who has given them power to become the children of God! My brethren, let us not stagger at the promise through unbelief, but believe up to the hilt!

Furthermore, *let us know the promises.* Should we not carry them at our fingers' ends? Should we not know them better than anything else? The promises should be the classics of believers. If you have not read the last new book, and have not heard the last Act of the Government, yet know right well what God the Lord hath said, and look to see his word made good. We ought to be so versed in Scripture as always to have at the tip of our tongue the promise which most exactly meets our case. We ought to be transcripts of Scripture: the divine promise should be as much written upon our hearts as upon the pages of the Book. It is a sad pity that any child of God should be unaware of the existence of the royal promise which would enrich him. It is pitiful for any one of us to be like the poor man, who had a fortune left him, of which he knew nothing, and therefore he went on sweeping a crossing, and begging for pence. That is the use of having an anchor at home when your ship is in a storm at sea? What avails a promise which you cannot remember so as to plead it in prayer? Whatever else you do not know, do endeavour to be familiar with those words of the Lord which are more needful to our souls than bread to our bodies.

Let us also make use of the promises. A little while ago, a friend gave me a cheque for certain charities, and he said to me, "Be sure that you pay it into the bank to-day." You may rest assured that this was done. I do not keep cheques to look at, and play with: they go to the banker's, and the cash is received and expended.

The precious promises of our great God are expressly intended to be taken to him, and exchanged for the blessings which they guarantee. Prayer takes the promise to the bank of Faith, and obtains the golden blessing. Mind how you pray. Make real business of it. Let it never be a dead formality. Some people pray a long time, but do not get what they are supposed to ask for, because they do not plead the promise in a truthful, business-like way. If you were to go into a bank, and stand an hour talking to the clerk, and then come out again without your cash, what would be the good of it? If I go to a bank, I pass my cheque across the counter, take up my money, and go about my business: that is the best way of praying. Ask for what you want, because the Lord has promised it. Believe that you have the blessing, and go forth to your work in full assurance of it. Go from your knees singing, because the promise is fulfilled: thus will your prayer be answered. It is not the length of your prayer, but the strength of your prayer which wins with God; and the strength of prayer lies in your faith in the promise which you have pleaded before the Lord.

Lastly, *talk about the promises*. Tell the King's household what the King has said. Never keep God's lamps under bushels. Promises are proclamations; exhibit them on the wall; read them aloud at the market-cross. Oh, that our conversation were more often sweetened with the precious promises of God! After dinner we often sit for half-an-hour, and pull our ministers to pieces, or scandalize our neighbors. How often is this the Sunday's amusement! It would be far better if we said, "Now, friend, quote a promise," and if the other replied, "And you mention a promise too." Then let each one speak according to his own personal knowledge concerning the Lord's fulfillment of those promises, and let every one present tell the story of the Lord's faithfulness to him. By such holy converse we should warm our own hearts, and gladden one another's spirits, and the Sabbath would thus be rightly spent.

Businessmen speak of their trade, travelers of their adventures, and farmers of their crops; should not we abundantly utter the memory of the Lord's goodness, and talk of his faithfulness? If we did so, we should all endorse Peter's statement, that our God has given unto us *"exceeding great and precious promises."*

XII.

THE LORD'S PROMISE— THE RULE OF HIS GIVING

"And the Lord gave Solomon wisdom, as he promised him." —I Kings 5:12

HOW the Lord wrought wisdom in Solomon I do not know; but he promised that he would give him wisdom, and he kept his word. The more you think of this the more remarkable will the fact appear. Solomon was not born under the most hopeful circumstances for wisdom. As the darling child of a somewhat aged father, he was highly likely to be spoiled. As a young man who came to a throne before he was at all fitted for it in the course of nature, he was very likely to have made great blunders and mistakes. As a man of strong animal passions, which in the end overpowered him, he seemed more likely to prove a profligate than a philosopher. As a person possessing great wealth, unlimited power, and unvarying prosperity, he had little of that trying experience by which men acquire wisdom. Who were his teachers? Who taught him to be wise? His penitent mother may have set before him much of sound morality and religion, but she could never have imparted to him the eminent degree of wisdom which raised him above all other men and set him upon the pinnacle of renown. He knew more than others, and therefore could not have borrowed his wisdom from them. Sages sat at his feet, and his fame brought pilgrims from the ends of the earth: none could have been his tutors, since he surpassed them all. How did this man rise to absolute preeminence in wisdom, so as to make his name throughout all time the synonym for a wise man?

It is a very mysterious process this creation of a master mind. Who shall give a young man wisdom? You can impart knowledge to him, but not wisdom. No tutor, no master, no divine, can give another man wisdom: he has much ado to get a little of it for himself. Yet God gave Solomon largeness of heart as the sands of the sea, and wisdom unrivaled; for God can do all things. By operations known only to himself, the Lord produced in the young king a capacity for observation, reasoning, and prudent action, seldom if ever equaled. We have often admired the wisdom of Solomon; I invite you still more to admire the wisdom of Jehovah, by whom Solomon's marvelous genius was produced.

The reason why the Lord wrought this wonder upon Solomon was *because he had promised to do it, and he is sure to keep his word.* Many another text would serve my turn as well as this one, for all I desire to bring out of it is this—that whatever God has promised to anyone, he will surely give it to him. Whether it be wisdom to Solomon, or grace to my reader, if the Lord has made the promise, he will not allow it to be a dead letter. The God who performed his word in this very remarkable instance, where the matter was so entirely beyond human power, and was surrounded with such disadvantageous circumstances, will accomplish his promise in other cases, however difficult and mysterious the process of performance may be. God will always keep his word to the letter; yea, and he will usually go beyond what the letter seems to mean. In this instance, while he gave Solomon wisdom, he also added to him riches, and a thousand other things which did not appear in the compact. "Seek ye first the kingdom of God and his righteousness, and all these things shall be added unto you." He who makes promises about infinite blessings, will throw in every-day things as if they were of small account, and were given in as a matter of course, like the grocer's paper and string with which he packs up our purchases.

From the case of Solomon, and thousands of a similar kind, we learn first that *the rule of God's giving is—as he has promised*.

The page of history sparkles with instances. The Lord promised to our fallen parents that the seed of the woman should bruise the serpent's head: behold, that wondrous Seed of the woman has appeared, and has gotten for himself, and for us, the glorious victory of our redemption! In the fulfillment of that one promise we have security for the keeping of all the rest. When God promised to Noah that entering into the ark he would be safe, he found it so. Not one of those innumerable waves which destroyed the antediluvian world, could break into his place of safety. When God said to Abraham that he would give him a seed, and a land which should be the possession of that seed, it seemed impossible; but Abraham believed God, and in due time rejoiced to behold Isaac, and to see in him the promised heir. When the Lord promised to Jacob that he would be with him and do him good, he kept his word, and gave him the deliverance for which he wrestled at the brook Jabbok, That long-slumbering promise, that the seed of Israel should possess the land which flowed with milk and honey; it did seem as if it would never be accomplished, when the tribes were reduced to slavery in Egypt, and Pharaoh held them with iron grip, and would not let them go. But God, who undertook for his people, brought them out with a high hand, and with an outstretched arm, on the very day in which he promised to rescue them. He divided the Red Sea also, and he led his people through the wilderness, for his people, brought them out with a high hand, and with an outstretched arm, on the very day in which he promised to rescue them. He divided the Red Sea also, and he led his people through the wilderness, for he assured them that he would do so. He clave the Jordan in twain, and he drove out the Canaanites before his people, and gave to Israel the land for their inheritance, even as he had promised. The histories of the Lord's faithfulness are so many, that time would fail us to repeat them all. God's words have always in due time been justified by God's acts. God has dealt with men according to his promise. Whenever they have taken hold upon the promise, and said, "Do as thou hast said," God has responded to the plea, and proved that it is no vain thing to trust him. Throughout all time it has been God's unvarying rule to keep his word to the letter, and to the moment.

"This is big talk," says one; then we will descend to smaller talk. *It is God's way to keep his promise to each individual.* We ourselves are living witnesses that God forgets not his word. Tens of thousands of us can testify that we have trusted in him and have never been confounded. I was once a broken-hearted sinner, cowering down beneath the black cloud of almighty wrath, guilty and self-condemned, and I felt that if I were banished for ever from Jehovah's presence, I could not say a word against the justice of the sentence. When I read in his word, "If we confess our sins, he is faithful and just to forgive us our sins," I went to him. Tremblingly I resolved to test his promise. I acknowledged my transgressions unto the Lord, and he forgave the iniquity of my sin. I am telling no idle tale, for the deep, restful peace which came to my heart in the moment of forgiveness was such that it seemed as if I had begun a new life; as, indeed, I had.

This is how it came about: I heard, one Sabbath day, a poor man speak upon that promise, "Look unto me, and by ye saved, all ye ends of the earth." I could not understand how a mere look at Christ could save me. It seemed too simple an act to effect so great a result; but, as I was ready to try anything, I LOOKED—*I looked to Jesus.*

It was all I did. It was all I could do. I looked unto him who is set forth as a propitiation for sin; and in a moment I saw that I was reconciled to God. I saw that if Jesus suffered in my stead, I could not suffer too; and that if he bore all my sin, I had no more sin to bear. My iniquity must be blotted out if Jesus bore it in my stead, and suffered all its penalty. With that thought there came into my spirit a sweet sense of peace with God through Jesus Christ my Lord. The promise was true, and I found it to be so. It happened some six-and-thirty years ago, but I have never lost the sense of that complete salvation which I then found, nor have I lost that peace which so sweetly dawned upon my spirit. *Since then I have never relied in vain upon a promise of God. I have been placed in positions of great peril, have known great need, have felt sharp pain, and have been weighted with incessant anxieties; but the Lord has been true to every line of his word, and when I have trusted him he has carried me through everything without a failure. I am bound to speak well of him, and I do so. TO THIS I SET MY HAND AND SEAL, without hesitation or reserve.*

The experience of all believers is too much the same effect: we began our new lives of joy and peace by believing the promise-making God, and we continue to live in the same manner. A long list of fulfilled promises is present to our happy memories, awakening our gratitude and confirming our confidence. We have tested the faithfulness of our God year after year, in a great many ways, but always with the same result. We have gone to him with promises of the common things of life, relating to daily bread, and raiment, and children, and home; and the lord has dealt graciously with us. We have resorted to him concerning sickness, and slander, and doubt, and temptation; and never has he failed us. In little things he has been mindful of us: even the hairs of our head have been numbered. When it appeared very unlikely that the promise could be kept, it has been fulfilled with remarkable exactness.

We have been broken down by the falseness of man, but we have exulted and do exult in the truthfulness of God. It brings the tears into our eyes to think of the startling ways in which Jehovah, our God, has wrought to carry out his gracious promises.

> "Thus far we prove that promise good,
> Which Jesus ratified with blood:
> Still he is faithful, wise, and just,
> And still in him believers trust."

Let me freely speak to all who trust in the Lord. Children of God, has not your heavenly Father been true to you? Is not this your constant experience, that you are always failing, but *he* never fails? Well said our apostle, "Though we believe not, he abideth faithful: he cannot deny himself." We may interpret divine language in its broadest sense, and we shall find that the Lord's promise is kept to the utmost of its meaning. The rule of his giving is large and liberal: the promise is a great vessel, and the Lord fills it to overflowing. As the Lord in Solomon's case gave him *"as he promised him,"* so will he in every instance so long as the world standeth. O reader! Believe the promise, and thus prove yourself to be an inheritor of it. May the Holy Spirit lead you thus to do, for Jesus' sake!

XIII.

THE RULE WITHOUT EXCEPTION

"Blessed be the Lord, that hath given rest unto his people Israel, according to all that he promised: there hath not failed one word of all his good promise, which he promised by the hand of Moses his servant." —Kings 8:56

God gives good things to men according to his promise. This is a matter of fact, and not a mere opinion. We declare it, and defy all the world to bring any evidence to disprove the statement.

Upon this point the writer is a personal witness. My experience has been long, and my observation has been wide; but I have never yet met with a person who trusted God, and found the Lord's promise fail him. I have seen many living men sustained under heavy trials by resting in the word of the Lord, and I have also seen many dying persons made triumphant in death by the same means; but I have never met with a believer who has been made ashamed of his hope because of his temporal afflictions, nor with one who on his deathbed has repented of trusting in the Lord. All my observation points the other way, and confirms me in the persuasion that the Lord is faithful to all who rely upon him. About this matter I should be prepared to make solemn affirmation in a court of justice. I would not utter a falsehood under the pretext of a pious fraud, but I would testify upon this important subject as an honest witness without reserve or equivocation. I never knew a man in the pangs of death lament that he trusted the Savior. Nay, what is more, I have never heard that such a thing has happened anywhere at any time. If there had been such a case, the haters of the gospel would have advertised it high and low; every street would have heard the evil news; every preacher would have been confronted with it. We should have been met with pamphlets at the door of every church and chapel, reporting that such an one, who had lived a saintly life, and relied on the Redeemer's merits, had discovered in his last hours that he had been duped, and that the doctrine of the cross was all delusion. We challenge opponents to discover such an instance. Let them find it among rich or poor, old or young. Let the very fiend himself, if he can, bear witness to the failure of a single promise of the Living God. But it has not been said that Jehovah has deceived one of his people, and it never shall be said; for God is true to every word that he has ever spoken.

God never stoops to a lie. The mere supposition is blasphemous. Why should he be false? What is there about him that could cause him to break his word? It would be contrary to his nature. How could he be God and not be just and true? He cannot therefore violate his promise through any want of faithfulness.

Furthermore, the Omnipotent God never promises beyond his power. We frequently intend to act according to our word, but we find ourselves mastered by overwhelming circumstances, and our promise falls to the ground because we are unable to perform it. It can never be so with the

Almighty God, for his ability is without limit. All things are possible with him.

Our promise may have been made in error, and we may afterwards discover that it would be wrong to do as we have said; but God is infallible, and therefore his word will never be withdrawn upon the ground of a mistake. Infinite wisdom has set its *imprimatur* upon every promise; each word of the Lord is registered by unerring judgment, and ratified by eternal truth.

Nor can the promise fail because of an alteration in the Divine Promiser. *We* change; poor, frail things that we are! But the Lord knows no variableness, neither shadow of a turning; hence his word abideth forever the same. Because he changes not, his promises stand fast like the great mountains. "Hath he said, and shall he not do it?" Our strong consolation rests upon the immutable things of God.

Nor can the word of the Lord fall to the ground through forgetfulness on his part. With our tongues *we* outrun our hands; for, although we are willing, we fail in the performing because other things come in, and distract our attention. We forget, or we grow cold; but never is it so with the Faithful Promiser. His most ancient promise is still fresh in his mind, and he means it now as he did when he first uttered it. He is, in fact, always giving the promise, since there is no time with him. The old promises of Scripture are new promises to faith; for every word still proceedeth out of the mouth of the Lord, to be bread for men.

Because of all this, the word of the Lord deserves all faith, both implicit and explicit. We can trust men too much, but we can never do so towards God. It is the surest thing that has been, or that can ever be. To believe his word is to believe what none can fairly question. Has God said it? Then so it must be. Heaven and earth will pass away, but God's word will never pass away. The laws of nature may be suspended: fire may cease to burn, and water to drown, for this would involve no unfaithfulness in God; but for his word to fail would involve a dishonouring variableness in the character and nature of the Godhead, and this can never be. Let us set to our seal that God is true, and never suffer a suspicion of his veracity to cross our minds.

The immutable word of promise is, and ever must be, the rule of God's giving. Consider a little, while I make a further observation, namely, that *against this no other rule can stand*. With the rule of God's promise no other law, supposed or real, can ever come into conflict.

The law of deserving is sometimes set up against it, but it cannot prevail. "Oh," says one, "I cannot think that God can or will save, for there is no good thing in me!" You speak rightly, and your fear cannot be removed if God is to act towards you upon the rule of deserving. But if you believe on his Son Jesus, that rule will not operate, for the Lord will act towards you according to the rule of his promise. The promise was not founded upon your merits; it was freely made, and it will be as freely kept. If you enquire how your ill-deservings can be met, let me remind you of Jesus who came to save you from your sins. The boundless deservings of the Lord Jesus are set to your account, and your terrible demerits are thereby neutralized one for all. The law of merit would sentence you to destruction as you stand in your own proper person; but he that believeth is not under law but under grace; and under grace the great Lord deals with men according to pure mercy as revealed in his promise. Choose not to be self-righteous, or justice must condemn you; be willing to accept salvation as a free gift bestowed through the exercise of the sovereign prerogative of God, who says, "I will have mercy on whom I will have mercy." Be humbly trustful in the grace of God which is revealed in Christ Jesus, and the promise shall be richly fulfilled to you.

Neither doth the Lord deal with men according to *the measure of their moral ability*. "Oh," says the seeker, "I think I might be saved if I could make myself better, or become more religious, or exercise greater faith; but I am without strength.

I cannot believe; I cannot repent; I cannot do anything aright!" Remember, then, that the Gracious God has not promised to bless you according to the measure of your ability to serve him, but according to the riches of his grace as declared in his word. If his gifts were bestowed according to your spiritual strength, you would get nothing; for you can do nothing without the Lord. But as the promise is kept according to the infinity of divine grace, there can be no question cast upon it. You need not stagger at the promise through unbelief, but reckon that he who has promised is able also to perform. Do not limit the Holy One of Israel by dreaming that his love is bounded by your capacity. The volume of the river is not to be computed by the dryness of the desert through which it flows: there is no logical proportion between the two. With half an eye one can see that there is no calculating the extent of infinite love by measuring human weakness. The operations of almighty grace are not limited by mortal strength, or want of strength. God's power will keep God's promise. It is not your weakness that can defeat God's promise, nor your strength that can fulfill the promise: he that spoke the word will himself make it good. It is neither your business nor mine to keep God's promises: that is his office, and not ours. Poor helpless one, attach your heavy wagon of incapacity to the great engine of the promise, and you will be drawn along the lines of duty and blessing! Though you are more dead than alive, though you have more weakness than strength, this shall not affect the certainty of the divine engagement. The power of the promise lies in him who made the promise. Look therefore away from self to God. If you are faint, swoon away upon the bosom of the divine promise; if you count yourself dead, be buried in the grave where lie the bones of a promise, and you shall be made alive as soon as you touch them. What we can or cannot do is not the question; but everything hinges upon what the Lord can do. It is enough for us to keep our own contracts without attempting to keep God's promises. I should not like my fellow-man to doubt my solvency because a beggar who lives in the next street cannot pay his debts. Why, then, should I suspect the Lord because I have grave cause to distrust myself? *My* ability is quite another question from the faithfulness of God, and it is a pity to mix the two things. Let us not dishonour our god by dreaming that *his* arm has waxed short because our arm has grown weak or weary.

Neither must we measure god by the rule of our feelings. Often do we hear the lamentation —"I do not feel that I can be saved. I do not feel that such sin as mine can be forgiven. I do not feel it possible that my hard heart can ever be softened and renewed." This is poor, foolish talk. In what way can our feelings guide us in such matters? Do you feel that the dead in their graves can be raised again? Do you even feel that the cold of winter will be followed by the heat of summer? How can you feel these things? You believe them. To talk of feeling in the matter is absurd. Does the fainting man feel that he will revive? Is it not the nature of such a state to suggest death? Do dead bodies feel that they will have a resurrection? Feeling is out of the question.

God gave Solomon wisdom as he had promised him, and he will give you what he has promised, whatever your feelings may be. If you look through the Book of Deuteronomy, you will see how often Moses uses the expression "*as he promised.*" He says (Deut. 1:11), "The Lord bless you as he hath promised you": h cannot pronounce on Israel a larger benediction. That holy man viewed the dealings of the lord with constant admiration, because they were "as he promised." In our case, also, the rule of the Lord's dealings will be "as he promised." Our experience of divine grace will not be "as we now feel," but "as he promised."

While writing thus for the comfort of others, I feel bound to confess that, personally, I am the subject of very changeful feelings; but I have learned to set very small store by them, either one way or the other: above all, I have ceased to estimate the truth of the promise by my condition of mind. Today I feel so joyful that I could dance to the tune of Miriam's timbrel; but perhaps when I wake tomorrow morning I shall only be able to sigh in harmony with Jeremiah's lamentations. Has my salvation changed according to these feelings? Then it must have had a very movable foundation. Feelings are more fickle than the winds, more unsubstantial than bubbles: are these to be the gauge of the divine fidelity? States of mind more or less depend upon the condition of the liver or the stomach: are we to judge the Lord by these? Certainly not. The state of the barometer may send our feelings up or down: can there be much dependence upon things so changeable? God does not suspend his eternal love upon our emotions; that were to build a temple on a wave. We are saved according to facts, not according to fancies. Certain eternal verities prove us saved or lost; and those verities are not affected by our exhilarations or depressions. O my reader, do not set up your feelings as a test by which to try the truthfulness of the Lord! Such conduct is a sort of mingled insanity and wickedness. If the Lord has said the word, he will make it good, whether you feel triumphant or despondent.

Again, *God will not give to us according to the rule of probabilities.* It does seem very improbable that you, my friend, should be blessed of the Lord that made heaven and earth; but if you trust the Lord you are favoured as surely as the Blessed Virgin herself, of whom it is said that all generations shall call her blessed; for it is written, "Blessed is she that believeth; for there shall be a performance of those things which were told her from the Lord." "O Lord of hosts, blessed is the man that trusteth in thee!" It may seem improbable that an old sinner, steeped in vice, should, by believing in Jesus, at once begin a new life; and yet it shall be so. It may seem very unlikely that a woman living in sin should hear that word, "He that believeth on him hath everlasting life," should immediately lay hold upon it, and at once receive everlasting life; yet it is true, for all that; and I have seen it so. Our God is a God of wonders. Things improbable, yea, impossible, with us, are everyday things with him. He causes the camel, despite its hump, to go through the needle's eye. He calleth the things which are not as though they were. Do you laugh at the very idea of your being saved? Let it not be the distrustful laugh of Sarah, but the joyous expectancy of Abraham. Believe on Jesus, and you shall laugh all over inwardly and outwardly, not from incredulity, but for quite another reason. When we know God we do not cease to wonder, but we begin to be at home with wonders. Believe the promise of God's grace, and believing, you shall live in a new world which shall be always wonder-land to you. It is a happy thing to have such faith in god as to expect as certain that which to mere human judgment is most unlikely. "With God all things are possible": it is therefore possible that he should have every soul that believeth in Jesus. The law of gravitation acts in all cases, and so does the law of divine faithfulness: there are no exceptions to the rule that God will keep his covenant. Extreme cases, difficult cases, yea, impossible cases, are included within the circle of the Lord's word, and therefore none need despair, or even doubt. God's opportunity has come when man's extremity is reached. The worse the case, the more sure is it to be helped of the Lord. Oh, that my hopeless, helpless reader would do the Lord the honour to believe him, and leave all in his hands!

How long will it be ere men will trust their God? "O thou of little faith, wherefore didst thou doubt?" Oh, that we would settle it in our minds that we would never again distrust the Faithful One!

"Let God be true, but every man a liar." The Lord himself saith, "Is the Lord's hand waxed short? Thou shalt see now whether my word shall come to pass unto thee or not" (Numbers 11:23). Let not the Lord speak thus to us in anger, but let us believe and be sure that the solemn declarations of the Lord must be fulfilled. Speak no longer one to another, saying, "What is truth?" but know infallibly that the word of the Lord is sure, and endureth for ever.

Here is a promise for the reader to begin with: let him test it, and see if it be not true: —"CALL UPON ME IN THE DAY OF TROUBLE: I WILL DELIVER THEE, AND THOU SHALT GLORIFY ME' (Psalm 50:15).

XIV.

TAKING POSSESSION OF THE PROMISE

"I am the Lord God of Abraham thy father, and the god of Isaac: the land whereon thou liest, to thee will I give it." –Genesis 28:13.

TIMOROUS souls find much difficulty in laying hold upon the promises of God as being made to themselves: they fear that it would be presumption to grasp things so good and precious. As a general rule, we may consider that *if we have faith to grasp a promise, that promise is ours.* He who gives us the key which will fit the lock of his door intends that we should open the door and enter. There can never be presumption in humbly believing God; there may be a great deal of it in daring to question his word. We are not likely to err in trusting the promise too far. Our failure lies in want of faith, not in excess of it. It would be hard to believe God too much: it is dreadfully common to believe him too little. "According to your faith be it unto you," is a benediction from which the Lord will never draw back. "If thou canst believe, all things are possible to him that believeth." It is written, "they could not enter in because of unbelief;" but it is never said that one who entered in by faith was censured for his impertinence, and driven out again.

Jacob, according to the text with which we have headed this chapter, took possession of the promised land by stretching himself upon it, and going to sleep. There is no surer way of taking possession of a promise than by placing your whole weight upon it, and then enjoying a hearty rest. *"The land whereon thou liest, to thee will I give it."*

How often have I found the promise true to my own self when I have accepted it as truth, and acted upon it! I have stretched myself upon it as upon a couch, and left myself in the hands of the Lord; and a sweet repose has crept over my spirit. Confidence in God realizes its own desires. The promise which our Lord made to those who seek favors in prayer runs thus, —"Believe that ye receive them, and ye shall have them." This sounds strange, but it is true; it is according to the philosophy of faith. Say, by a realizing faith, "this promise is mine," and straightway it is yours. It is by faith that we "receive promises", and not by sight and sense.

The promises of God are not enclosures to be the private property of this saint or that, but they are an open common for all the dwellers in the parish of Holy Faith. No doubt there are persons who would, if they could, make a freehold of the stars, and a personal estate out of the sun and moon. The same greed might put a ring-fence around the promises; but this cannot be done. As well might misers hedge in the song-birds, and claim the music of lark and thrush as their own sole inheritance, as propose to keep promises all to themselves. No, not the best of the saints can, even if they wished to do so, put a single word of the God of grace under lock and key. The promise is not only "unto you, and to your children," but also "to all that are afar off, even as many as the Lord our God shall call." What a comfort is this! Let us take up our common-rights, and possess by faith what the Lord has made ours by a covenant of salt.

Words spoken to Jacob belong equally to all believers. Hosea says of him, "Yea, he had power over the angel, and prevailed: he found him in Bethel, *and there he spake with us.*" So that Jehovah spake with us when he spake with the patriarch. The wonders which God displayed at the Red Sea were wrought for all his people, for we read, *"there did we rejoice in him."* (See Psalm 66:6.) It is true we were not there, and yet the joy of Israel's victory is ours. The apostle quotes the word of the Lord to Joshua as if it were spoken to any and every child of God,—"He hath said I will never leave *thee* nor forsake *thee*" (Hebrews 13:5), the fact being that no word of the Lord ends with the occasion which called it forth, or spends itself in blessing the individual to whom it was first addressed. All the promises are to believers who have faith enough to embrace them, and plead them at the throne of grace. What God is to one who trusts him, he will be to all such according to their circumstances and necessities.

The Bible has its eye upon each one of us as it utters its words of grace. A Bampton lecturer has well said, "We, ourselves, and such as we are, are the very persons who Scripture speaks of; and to whom, as men, in every variety of persuasive form, it makes its condescending, though celestial, appeal. The point worthy of observation is, to note how a book of its description and its compass should possess this versatility of power, this eye, like that of a portrait uniformly fixed upon us, turn where we will."

> "Eye of God's word! where'er we turn,
>
> Ever upon us thy kind gaze
>
> Doth all our depths of woe discern,
>
> Unravel every bosom's maze."
>
> What word is this? Whence know'st thou me?
>
> All wondering cries the humbled heart,

To hear thee that deep mystery,

This singular personality of the word to each one of a thousand generations of believers is one of its greatest charms, and one of the surest proofs of its divine inspiration. We treat our Bibles, not as old almanacs, but as books for the present, new, fresh, adapted for the hour. Abiding sweetness dwells in undiminished freshness in the ancient words upon which our fathers fed in their day. Glory be to God, we are feasting on them still; or if not, we ought to be; and can only blame ourselves if we do not!

The wells of Abraham served for Isaac, and Jacob, and a thousand generations. Come, let us let down our buckets, and with joy draw water out of the old wells of salvation, digged in the far-off days when our fathers trusted in the Lord, and he delivered them! We need not fear that we shall be superstitious or credulous. The promises of the Lord are made to all who will believe them: faith is itself a warrant for trusting. If thou *canst* trust, thou mayest trust. After being fulfilled hundreds of times, the words of promise still stand to be yet further made good. Many a time and oft have we stooped down to the spring-head in the meadow, and quaffed a cooling draught; it is just as full and free, and we may drink today with as much confidence as if we now stooped for the first time. Men do not keep their promises over and over again: it would be unreasonable to expect it of them. They are cisterns, but thou, O Lord, art a fountain! All my fresh springs are in thee.

Come, reader imitate Jacob! As he laid him down in a certain place, and took of the stones of the place for his pillows, so do thou. Here is the whole Bible for a couch, and here are certain promises to serve as pillows; lay down thy burdens, and thyself also, and take thy rest. Behold, this Scripture and its promises are henceforth thine,—*"the land whereon thou liest, to thee will I give it."*

XV.

ENDORSING THE PROMISE

"I believe God, that it shall be even as it was told me."
–Acts 27:25.

PAUL had received a special promise, and he openly avowed his faith in it. He believed that God would fulfill every detail of that promise. In this way he set to his seal that God is true. We are each one of us bound to do this with those words of the Lord which are suitable to our case. This is what I mean by the head-line—*endorsing the promise.*

A friend gives me for the Orphanage a cheque, which runs thus, "Pay to the order of C.H. Spurgeon, the sum of L10." His name is good, and his bank is good, but I get nothing from his kindness till I put my own name at the back of his cheque or draft. It is a very simple act: I merely sign my name, and the banker pays me: but the signature cannot be dispensed with.

There are many nobler names than mine, but none of these can be used instead of my own. If I wrote the Queen's name, it would not avail me. If the Chancellor of the Exchequer placed his signature on the back of the document, it would be in vain. I must myself affix my own name. Even so, each one must personally accept, adopt, and endorse the promise of God by his own individual faith, or he will derive no benefit from it.

If you were to write Miltonic lines in honour of the bank, or exceed Tennyson in verses in praise of the generous benefactor of the orphans, it would avail nothing. The choicest language of men and of angels would count for nothing; what is absolutely requisite is the personal signature of the party who is named as the receiver. However fine might be the sketch which an artistic pencil might draw upon the back of the draft, that also would be of no sort of service: the simple, self-written name is demanded, and nothing will be accepted instead of it. We must believe the promise, each one for himself, and declare that we know it to be true, or it will bring us no blessing. No good works, or ceremonial performances, or rapturous feelings, can supply the place of a simple confidence. "He that cometh to God *must* believe that he is, and that he is a rewarder of them that diligently seek him." Some things may be or may not be, but this *must* be.

The promise may be said to run thus, "I promise to pay to the order of any sinner who will believe on me the blessing of eternal life." The sinner *must* write his name on the back of the draft; but nothing else is asked of him. He believes the promise, he goes to the throne of grace with it, and he looks to receive the mercy which it guaranteed to him. He shall have that mercy: he cannot fail to do so. It is written, "He that believeth on the Son hath everlasting life"; and so it is.

Paul believed that all in the ship with him would escape *because God had promised it*. He accepted the promise as ample security for the fact, and acted accordingly. He was calm amid the storm; he gave his comrades sage and sensible advice as to breaking their fast; and, in general, he managed matters as a man would do who was sure of a happy escape from the tempest. Thus he treated God as he should be treated, namely, with unquestioning confidence. An upright man likes to be trusted; it would grieve him if he saw that he was regarded with suspicion. Our faithful God is jealous of his honour, and cannot endure that men should treat him as if he could be false. Unbelief provokes the Lord above any other sin; it touches the apple of his eye and cuts him to the quick. Far be it from us to perpetrate so infamous a wrong towards our heavenly Father; let us believe him up to the hilt, placing no bounds to our hearty reliance upon his word.

Paul openly avowed his confidence in the promise. It is well that we should do the same. Just at this time, bold, outspoken testimonies to the truth of God are greatly needed, and may prove to be of seven-fold value. The air is full of doubt; indeed, few really and substantially believe. Such a man as George Muller, who believes in God for the mainte-nance of two thousand children, is a rare personage. "When the Son of man cometh, shall he find faith on the earth?" Therefore let us speak out. Infidelity has defied us; let no man's heart fail him, but let us meet the giant with the sling and stone of actual experience, and unflinching witness. God does keep his promise, and we know it. We dare endorse every one of his promises. Ay, we would do it with our blood if it were needful! The word of the Lord endureth for ever, and of this we are undaunted witnesses, even all of us who are called by his name.

XVI.

> ## THE PROMISE USED
> ## FOR THIS LIFE

"Godliness is profitable unto all things, having promise of the life that now is, and of that which is to come."

I Tim. 4:8

A SORT of affectation prevents some Christians from treating religion as if its sphere lay among the common places of daily life. It is to them transcendental and dreamy; rather a creation of pious fiction than a matter of fact. They believe in God, after a fashion, for things spiritual, and for the life which is to be; but they totally forget that true godliness hath the promise of the life which now is, as well as of that which is to come. To them it would seem almost a profanation to pray about the small matters of which daily life is made up. Perhaps they will be startled if I venture to suggest that this should make them question the reality of their faith. If it cannot bring them help in little troubles of life, will it support them in the greater trials of death? If it cannot profit them as to food and raiment, what can it do for them as to the immortal spirit?

In the life of Abraham we perceive that his faith had to do with all the events of his earthly pilgrimage; it was connected with his removals from one country to another, with the separation of a nephew from his camp, with fighting against invaders, and specially with the birth of the long-promised son. No part of the patriarch's life was outside the circle of his faith in God. Towards the close of his life it is said, "and the Lord had blessed Abraham in all things," which includes temporals as well as spirituals. In Jacob's case the Lord promised him bread to eat, and raiment to put on, and the bringing of him to his father's house in peace; and all these things are of a temporal and earthly character. Assuredly these first believers did not spirit away the present blessings of the covenant, or regard it as an airy, mystical matter to believe in God. One is struck with the want of any line of demarcation between secular and sacred in their lives; they journeyed as pilgrims, fought like Crusaders, ate and drank like saints, lived as priests, and spake as prophets. Their life was their religion, and their religion was their life. They trusted God, not merely about certain things of higher import, but about everything, and thence, even a servant from one of their houses, when he was sent on an errand, prayed, "O Lord God of my master, prosper the way which I go!" This was genuine faith, and it is ours to imitate it, and no longer to allow the substance of the promise, and the life of faith, to evaporate in mere sentimental and visionary fancies. If trust in God is good for anything, it is good for everything within the line of the promise, and it is certain that the life which now is lies within that region.

Let my reader observe and practically use such words of God as these,—"Ye shall serve the Lord your God, and he shall bless thy bread, and thy water; and I will take sickness away from the midst of thee" (Ex. 23:25). "Trust in the Lord, and do good; so shalt thou dwell in the land, and verily thou shalt be fed")Ps. 37:3). "Surely he shall deliver thee from the snare of the fowler, and from the noisome pestilence. He shall cover thee with his feathers, and under his wings shalt thou trust: his truth shall be thy shield and buckler. Thou shalt not be afraid for the terror by night; nor for the arrow that flieth by day; nor for the pestilence that walketh in darkness; nor for the destruction that wasteth at noonday. A thousand shall fall at thy side, and ten thousand at they right hand; but it shall not come nigh thee" (Ps. 91:3-7). "He shall deliver thee in six troubles: yea, in seven there shall no evil touch thee" (Job 5:19. "He that walketh righteously, and speaketh uprightly; he that despiseth the gain of oppressions, that shaketh his hands from holding of bribes, that stoppeth his ears from hearing of blood, and shutteth his eyes from seeing evil; he shall dwell on high: his place of defence shall be the munitions of rocks: bread shall be given him; his waters shall be sure" (Is. 33:15,16). "For the Lord God is a sun and shield: the Lord will give grace and glory: no good thing will he withhold from them that walk uprightly" (Ps. 84:11). "No weapon that is formed against thee shall prosper; and every tongue that shall rise against thee in judgment thou shalt condemn. This is the heritage of the servants of the Lord, and their righteousness is of me, saith the Lord""(Is. 54:17).

Our Savior intended faith to be our *quietus* concerning daily cares, or he would not have said, "Therefore I say unto you, take no thought for your life, what ye shall eat, or what ye shall drink; nor yet for your body, what ye shall put on. Is not the life more than meat, and the body than raiment? Behold the fowls of the air: for they sow not, neither do they reap, nor gather into barns; yet your heavenly Father feedeth them. Are ye not much better than they?" (Matt. 6:25,26). What else but the exercise of faith concerning temporal things could he have meant when he used the following language? –"And seek not ye what ye shall eat, or what ye shall drink, neither be ye of doubtful mind. For all these things do the nations of the world see after: and your Father knoweth that ye have need of these things" (Luke 12:29,30).

Paul meant the same when he wrote, "Be careful for nothing; but in every thing by prayer and supplication with thanksgiving let your requests be made known unto God. And the peace of God, which passeth all understanding, shall keep your hearts and minds through Christ Jesus" (Phil. 4:6,7).

He who is gone to prepare heaven for us will not leave us without provision for the journey thither. God does not give us heaven as the Pope gave England to the Spanish King –*if he could get it:* but he makes the road sure, as well as the end. Now, our earthly necessities are as real as our spiritual ones, and we may rest sure that the Lord will supply them. He will send us those supplies in the way of promise, prayer, and faith, and so make them a means of education for us. He will fit us for Canaan by the experience of the wilderness.

To suppose that temporal things are too little for our condescending God, is to forget that he observes the flight of sparrows, and counts the hairs of his people's heads. Besides, everything is so little to him, that, if he does not care for the little, he cares for nothing. Who is to divide affairs by size or weight? The turning-point of history may be a minute circumstance. Blessed is the man to whom nothing is too small for God; for certainly nothing is too small to cause us sorrow, or to involve us in peril. A man of God once lost a key: he prayed about it, and found it. It was reported of him as a strange circumstance. Indeed, it was nothing unusual: some of us pray about everything, and tremble lest the infinitesimal things should not be sanctified by the word of God and prayer. It is not the including of trifles which is any trouble to our consciences, but the omission of them. We are assured that, when our Lord gave his angels charge to guard our feet from stones in the way, he placed all the details of our life under heavenly care, and we are glad to commit all things to his keeping.

It is one of the abiding miracles of the present dispensation that in Christ we have continual peace under all trials, and through him we have power in prayer to obtain from the lord all things necessary for this life and godliness. It has been the writer's lot to test the Lord hundreds of times about temporal needs, being driven thereto by the care of orphans and students. Prayer has many, many times brought opportune supplies, and cleared away serious difficulties. I know that faith can fill a purse, provide a meal, change a hard heart, procure a site for a building, heal sickness, quiet insubordination, and stay an epidemic. Like money in the worldling's hand, faith in the hand of the man of God "answereth all things." All things in heaven, and earth, and under the earth, answer to the command of prayer. Faith is not to be imitated by a quack, nor simulated by a hypocrite; but where it is real, and can grasp a divine promise with firm grip, it is a great wonder-worker. How I wish that my reader would so believe in god as to lean upon him in all the concerns of his life! This would lead him into a new world, and bring to him such confirmatory evidence as to the truth of our holy faith that we would laugh skeptics to scorn. Child-like faith in God provides sincere hearts with a practical prudence, which I am inclined to call—a sanctified common-sense. The simple-minded believer, though laughed at as an idiot, has a wisdom about him which cometh from above, and effectually baffles the cunning of the wicked. Nothing puzzles a malicious enemy like the straightforward unguardedness of an out-and-out believer.

He that believes his God is not afraid of evil tidings, for his heart has found a calm fixity in trusting in the Lord. In a thousand ways this faith sweetens, enlarges, and enriches life. Try it, dear reader, and see if it does not yield you an inmeasurable wealth of blessedness! It will not save you from trouble, for the promise is, "These things I have spoken unto you, that in me ye might have peace. In the world ye shall have tribulation: but be of good cheer; I have overcome the world" (John 16:33): but it will cause you to glory in tribulations also, "knowing that tribulation worketh patience; and patience, experience; and experience, hope: and hope maketh not ashamed; because the love of God is shed abroad in our hearts by the Holy Ghost which is given unto us"

(Rom. 5:3-5).

My faith not only flies to heaven,
But walks with God below;

To me are all things daily given,
While passing to and fro.
The promise speaks of worlds above,
But not of these alone;
It feeds and clothes me *now* with love,
And makes this world my own.
I trust the Lord, and he replies,
In things both great and small.
He honours faith with prompt supplies;
Faith honours *him* in all.

XVII.

SEARCHING OUT THE PROMISE

"Thou hast promised this goodness unto thy servant."
–II Samuel 7:28

KING David knew what the Lord had engaged to give him, and he referred to it specially in his prayer as "this good thing." *(Revised Version.)* We greatly need to be more definite in our supplications than we usually are: we pray for everything in such a way that we practically pray for nothing. It is well to know what we want. Hence our Lord said to the blind man, "What wilt thou that I should do unto thee?" He wished him to be aware of his own needs, and to be filled with earnest desires concerning those needs: these are valuable ingredients in the composition of prayer.

Knowing what we need, the next business is to find that the lord has promised us this particular blessing, for then we can go to God with the utmost confidence, and look for the fulfillment of his word. To this end we would diligently search the Scriptures, looking much to the cases of other believers which are like our own, and endeavouring to light upon that particular utterance of divine grace which is suitable to ourselves in our present circumstances. The more exact the agreement of the promise to the case, the greater the comfort which it will yield. In this school the believer will learn the value of plenary, ay, of verbal inspiration; for in his own instance he may have to dwell upon slight a matter as the number of a noun, as Paul did when quoting the promise made to Abraham he remarks, "Now to Abraham and his *seed* were the promises made. He saith not, And to *seeds*, as of many; but as of one, and to thy *seed*, which is Christ: (Gal. 3:16).

We may rest assured that somewhere in the inspired page there is a promise fitting the occasion. The infinite wisdom of God is seen in his having given us a revelation which meets the innumerable varieties of his people's conditions. Not a single trial is overlooked, however peculiar it may be. As there is food specially adapted for every living thing upon the face of the earth, so there is suitable support for every child of God in the volume of inspiration. If we do not find a fitting promise, it is because we do not look for it; or having found it, have not yet perceived its full meaning.

A homely comparison may be useful here. You have lost the key of a chest, and after trying all the keys you possess, you are obliged to send out for a smith. The tradesman comes with a huge bunch of keys of all sorts and sizes. To you they appear to be a singular collection of rusty instruments. He looks at the lock, and then he tries first one key and then another. He has not touched it yet; and your treasures are still out of your reach. Look, he has found a likely key: it almost touches the bolt, but not quite. He is evidently on the right tract now. At last the chest is opened, for the right key has been found. This is a correct representation of many a perplexity. You cannot get at the difficulty so as to deal with it aright, and find your way to a happy result. You pray, but have not the liberty in prayer which you desire. A definite promise is what you want. You try one and another of the inspired words, but they do not fit. The troubled heart sees reasons to suspect that they are not strictly applicable to the case in hand, and so they are left in the old Book for use another day; for they are not available in the present emergency. You try again, and in due season a promise presents itself, which seems to have been made for the occasion; it fits as exactly as a well-made key fits the wards of the lock for which it was originally prepared. Having found the identical word of the living God, you hasten to plead it at the throne of grace, saying, "O my Lord, thou hast promised this good thing unto thy servant; be pleased to grant it!" The matter is ended; sorrow is turned to joy; prayer is heard.

Frequently the Holy Spirit brings to our remembrance with life and power words of the Lord which else we might have forgotten. He also sheds a new light upon well-remembered passages, and so reveals a fullness in them which we had little suspected. In cases known to me, the texts have been singular, and for a while the person upon whose mind they were impressed could hardly see their bearing. For years one heart was comforted with the words "His soul shall dwell at ease; and his seed shall inherit the earth." This passage was seldom out of his mind; indeed, it seemed to him to be perpetually whispered in his ear. The special relation of the promise to his experience was made known by the event. A child of God, who mourned his years of barrenness, was lifted at once into joy and peace by that seldom-quoted word, "I will restore to you the years that the locust hath eaten." The bitter experiences of David as to slander and malice led to the utterance of consoling promises, which have been a thousand times appropriated by obscure and broken-hearted Christians when afflicted with "trials of cruel mockings." Before this dispensation shall close, we doubt not that every sentence of Scripture will have been illustrated by the life of one or other of the saints. Perhaps some obscure, and little-understood promise is still lying by until he shall come for whom it was specially written. If we may so say, there is one trusty key on the bunch which has not yet found its lock; but it will find it before the history of the church is finished: we may be sure of that.

The word of the Lord which would remove our present discomfort may be close at hand, and yet we may not be aware of it. With singular knowledge of human experience, John Bunyan represents the prisoner of Doubting Castle as finding in his own bosom the key called Promise, which opened every door in that gloomy prison-house. We often lie in durance vile when the means of obtaining fullest liberty proffers itself to us. If we would but open our eyes, we should, like Hagar, see a well of water close at hand, and wonder why we thought of dying of thirst. At this moment, O tempted brother, there is a word of the Lord awaiting thee! As the manna fell early in the morning, and lay ready for the Israelites to gather it as soon as ever they left their beds, so does the promise of the Lord wait for thy coming. The oxen and the fatlings of grace are killed, and all things are ready for thine immediate comfort. The mountain is full of chariots of fire, and horses of fire, prepared for thy deliverance; the prophet of the Lord can see them, and if thine eyes were opened thou wouldest see them too. Like the lepers at the gate of Samaria, it would be foolish for thee to sit where thou art, and die. Bestir thyself, for close at hand lavish mercy is poured forth, exceeding abundantly above all that thou dost ask or even think. Only believe, and enter into rest.

For the poor, the sick, and faint, the erring, there are words of good cheer which they alone can enjoy. For the fallen, the desponding, the despairing, the dying, there are cordials which are compounded with an eye to their peculiar maladies. The widow and the fatherless have their promises, and so have captives, travelers, shipwrecked mariners, aged persons, and those in the article of death. No one ever wanders where a promise does not follow him. An atmosphere of promise surrounds believers as the air surrounds the globe. I might almost call it omnipresent, and say of it, "Thou has beset me behind and before, and laid thine hand upon me. Such knowledge is too wonderful for me; it is high, I cannot attain unto it. Whither shall I go from thy spirit? Or whither shall I glee from thy presence?" (Ps. 139:5,6,7.) No depth of darkness can hide us from the covenant of promise; say, rather, in its presence the night shineth as the day. Wherefore, let us take courage, and by faith and patience wait in the land of our exile till the day of our home-bringing. So shall we, like the rest of the heirs of salvation, "inherit the promise."

Certain covenant engagements, made with the Lord Jesus Christ, as to his elect and redeemed ones, are altogether without condition so far as we are concerned; but many other wealthy words of the Lord contain stipulations which must be carefully regarded, or we shall not obtain the blessing. One part of my reader's diligent search must be directed towards this most important point. God will keep his promise to thee; only see thou to it that the way in which he conditions his engagement is carefully observed of thee. Only when we fulfill the requirement of a conditional promise can we expect that promise to be fulfilled to us. He hath said, "He that believeth in Jesus shall be saved." If thou believest in the Lord Jesus Christ, it is certain that thou shalt be saved; but no else. In the same way, if the promise is made to prayer, to holiness, to reading the word, to abiding in Christ, or whatever else it may be, give thy heart and soul to the thing commanded, that the blessing may become thine. In some cases, great blessedness is not realized because known duties are neglected. The promise cannot enter because "sin lieth at the door." Even an unknown duty may whip us with "a few stripes," and a few strokes may greatly mar our happiness. Let us endeavour to know the Lord's will in all things, and then let us obey it without a trace of hesitation. It is not of the way of our willfulness, but of the tracks of divine wisdom that we read, "Her ways are ways of pleasantness, and all her paths are peace."

Do not undervalue the grace of the promise because it has a condition appended to it; for, as a rule, it is in this way made doubly valuable,—the condition being in itself another blessing, which the Lord has purposely made inseparable from that which thou desirest, that thou mayest gain two mercies while seeking only one. Moreover, remember that the condition is grievous to those only who are not heirs of the promise: to them it is as a thorn hedge, keeping them off from the comfort to which they have no right; but to thee it is not grievous, but pleasant, and it is therefore no hindrance to thine access to the blessing. Those requirements, which show a black cloud and darkness to the Egyptians, have a bright side for the Israelites, and give light by night to them. To us the Lord's yoke is easy, and in taking it upon us we find rest unto our souls. See then that thou note the wording of the promise, and carry out all its precepts, that all good things may come to thee.

If thou art a believer in the Lord Jesus, all the promises are thine; and among them is one for this very day of the month, and for this particular place wherein thou art now encamped: wherefore search the roll of thy Magna Charta, and find out thy portion for this hour. Of all the promises which the Lord hath given in his book, he hath said, "No one of these shall fail, none shall want its mate, for my mouth hath commanded them." Therefore trust, and be not afraid. What ever else may prove a failure, the promise of God never will. Treasure laid up in this bank is beyond all hazard. "It is better to trust in the Lord than to put confidence in princes." Let us sing at every remembrance of the God of truth and grace.

"Tell of his wondrous faithfulness,
    And sound his power abroad;
Sing the sweet promise of his grace,
    And the performing God.
He that can dash whole worlds to death,
    And make them when he please;
He speaks, and that almighty breath
    Fulfills his great decrees.
His very word of grace is strong
    As that which built the skies;
The voice that rolls the stars along
    Speaks all the promises.

XVIII.

THE TIME OF THE PROMISE

"The time of the promise drew nigh." –Acts 7:17

THOMAS BROOKS reminds us that the mercies of God are not styled the *swift,* but "the *sure* mercies of David." There is nothing of hurry about the procedure of the Lord: it may even seem that the chariots of his grace are long in coming. It is by no means an unusual circumstance for the saints to be heard crying, "O Lord, how long?" It is written "the glory of the Lord shall be thy rearward" (Is. 58:8). Now the guard of the rear comes up last, but it does come. God may sometimes make us wait; but we shall see in the end that he is as surely the Omega as the Alpha of his peoples' salvation. Let us never distrust him, but though the vision tarry, let us wait for it; because it will surely come, it will not tarry (Hab. 2:3).

There once sailed from the port of London a vessel, which the owner called the *Swift-sure,* because he hoped it would prove both safe and speedy. Truly this is a fit name for the Lord's mercy; it is both swift and sure. David may not have said so in the text which Brooks quotes, but he often said as much and even more in others. Did he not say "He rode upon a cherub, and did fly; yea, he did fly upon the wings of the wind"? The Lord is not slow to hear the cries of his people. He has a set time to favour Zion, and when that set time is come there will be no delay.

The date for this fulfillment is an important part of a promise; indeed, it enters into the essence of it. It would be unjust to delay the payment of a debt; and the obligation to keep one's word is of the same nature. The Lord is prompt to the moment in carrying out his gracious engagements. The Lord had threatened to destroy the world with a flood, but he waited the full time of respite until Noah had entered the ark; and then, on the selfsame day, the fountains of the great deep were broken up. He had declared that Israel should come out of Egypt, and it was so: "And it came to pass at the end of the four hundred and thirty years, even the selfsame day it came to pass, that all the hosts of the Lord went out from the land of Egypt" (Exodus 12:41). According to Daniel, the Lord numbers the years of his promise, and counts the weeks of his waiting. As for the greatest promise of all, namely, the sending of his Son from heaven, the Lord was not behind-hand in that great gift, "but when the fullness of the time was come, God sent forth his Son, made of a woman." Beyond all question, the lord our God keeps his word to the moment.

When we are in need, we may be urgent with the Lord to come quickly to our rescue, even as David pleaded in the seventieth Psalm,—"Make haste, O God, to deliver me; make haste to help me, O Lord." (Verse 1.) "I am poor and needy: make haste unto me, O God: thou art my help and my deliverer; O Lord, make no tarrying." (Verse 5.) The Lord even condescends to describe himself as making speed to carry out his gracious engagements, saying, "I the Lord will hasten it in his time" (Isaiah 60:22). But we must not pray in this fashion as though we had the slightest fear that the Lord could or would be dilatory, or that he needed us to quicken his diligence. No. "The Lord is not slack concerning his promise, as some men count slackness" (II Peter 3:9). Our God is slow to anger, but in deeds of grace "his word runneth very swiftly" (Psalm 147:15). Sometimes his speed to bless his people outstrips time and thought: as, for instance, when he fulfills that ancient declaration, "It shall come to pass, that before they call, I will answer; and while they are yet speaking, I will hear" (Isaiah 65:24).

Yet there are delays in the answers to our prayers. As the husbandman does not reap today that which he sowed yesterday, so neither do we always at once obtain from the Lord that which we seek of him. The door of grace does open, but not to our first knocks. Why is this? It is because the mercy will be all the greater for being longer on the road. There is a time for every purpose under heaven, and everything is best in its time. Fruit ripens in its season; and the more seasonable it is the better it is. Untimely mercies would be only half mercies; therefore the Lord withholds them till they have come to their perfection. Even heaven itself will be all the better because it will not be ours till it is prepared for us, and we are prepared for it.

Love presides over the arrangements of grace, and strikes upon the bell when the best moment has arrived. God blesses us by his temporary delays, as well as by his prompt replies. We are not to doubt the Lord because his time has not yet come: that would be to act like petulant children, who must have a thing at the instant, or else they think they shall never have it. A waiting God is the true object of confidence to his waiting people. "Therefore will the Lord wait, that he may be gracious unto you" (Is. 30:18). His compassions fail not even when his gracious operations appear to be suspended, and our griefs are deepened. Yea, it is because he loves us so much that he tries us by delaying his answers of peace. It is with our Father in heaven even as it was with our Lord on earth: "Now Jesus loved Martha, and her sister, and Lazarus. When he had heard therefore that he was sick, he abode two days still in the same place where he was: (John

11:5,6). Love closes the hand of divine bounty, and restrains the outflow of favour, when it sees that a solid gain will ensue from a period of trial.

Perhaps the time of the promise has not yet come, because our trial has not yet fulfilled its design. The chastening must answer its purpose, or it cannot be brought to an end. Who would desire to see the gold taken out of the fire before its dross is consumed? Wait, O precious thing, till thou hast gained the utmost of purity! These furnace moments are profitable. It would be unwise to shorten such golden hours. The time of the promise corresponds with the time most enriching to heart and soul.

Perhaps, moreover, we have not yet displayed sufficient submission to the divine will. Patience has not yet had her perfect work. The weaning process is not accomplished: we are still hankering after the comforts which the Lord intends us forever to outgrow. Abraham made a great feast when his son Issac was weaned; and, peradventure, our heavenly Father will do the same with us. Lie low, proud heart! Quit thine idols; forsake thy fond dotings; and the promised peace will come unto thee.

Possibly, also, we have not yet performed a duty which will become the turning-point of our condition. The Lord turned again the captivity of Job when he prayed for his friends. It may be that the Lord will make us useful to a relative or other friend before he will favour us with personal consolations: we are not to see the face of our Joseph except our brother be with us. Some ordinance of the Lord's house may lie neglected, or some holy work may be left undone; and this may hinder the promise. Is it so? "Are the consolations of God small with thee? Is there any secret thing with thee? Peradventure we are yet to vow unto the Lord, and make a notable sacrifice unto him, and then will he bring his covenant to mind. Let his not have to complain, "Thou has brought me no sweet cane with money." Rather let us accept his challenge, "Bring ye all the tithes into the storehouse, and prove me now herewith, saith the Lord of hosts, if I will not open you the windows of heaven, and pour you out a blessing" (Mal. 3:10).

God's promises are so dated as to secure his glory in their fulfillment, and this must be enough for us when we can see no other reason for delay. It may be necessary for us to be made more fully aware of our need, and the great value of the blessings which we crave. That which too lightly comes may be too lightly prized. Perhaps our ungrateful spirits need tutoring to thankfulness by an education of waiting. We might not loudly sing if we did not deeply sigh. Wanting and waiting lead to panting and pleading; and these in due time lead to joying and rejoicing.

If all things could be known to us as they are known to God, we should bless him with all our hearts for keeping us under the smarting rod, and not sparing us for our crying. If we could know the end as well as the beginning, we should praise the Lord for closed doors, and frowning looks, and unanswered petitions. Surely, if we knew that the Lord's great purposes were answered by our continuing without the pleasures we desire, and bearing the evils which we dread, we should cry aloud to be left in our poverty, and to be shut up in our pain. If we can glorify God by being denied what we seek, we desire to be denied. Greatest of all our prayers, and sum of all the rest, is this one, "Nevertheless, not as I will, but as thou wilt."

XVIX.

The Promise in Possession Through the Spirit

"That holy Spirit of promise, which is the earnest of our inheritance until the redemption of the purchased possession, unto the praise of his glory." —Eph. 1:13,14

IN a very true and real sense the things promised in the covenant are already the property of believers. "All things *are* yours." The great Father might truly say to each one of the sons who abide in his house, "All that I have is thine." The inheritance is already ours, say the old divines, *in promisso, in pretio, in principiis;* that is to say, in the promise of God, in the price paid by the Lord Jesus, and in its first principles which are infused into us by the Holy Spirit. In his sure promise the Father has already "blessed us with all spiritual blessings in heavenly places in Christ": he has not only resolved to enrich us in the future, but even now he has endowed us with the treasures of his love. The Lord Jesus has not merely made us heirs of an infinite estate in the ages to come, but he has brought us into immediate enjoyment of a present portion; as saith the Scripture, "In whom also we have obtained an inheritance."

The Holy Spirit is in many ways the means of making the promised heritage ours even now. *By him se are "sealed."* We know of a surety that the inheritance is ours, and that we ourselves belong to the great Heir of all things. The operations of the Holy Ghost upon us in our regeneration, and his abiding in us by sanctification, are certificates of our being in grace, and of our being inheritors of glory. Beyond all other testimonies of our being saved, there stands this sure and certain evidence, namely, that the Spirit of the living God rests upon us. Repentance, faith, spiritual life, holy desires, upward breathings, and even "groanings which cannot be uttered." Are all proofs that the Holy Ghost is working upon us; and working in a way peculiar to the heirs of salvation. Life breathed into us by the Holy Ghost is the great seal of the kingdom of God to our souls. We need no dreams, nor visions, nor mystic voices, nor rapturous feelings: the quickening and renewing of the Holy Ghost are better seals than these. The Spirit of promise does not prepare men for a blessedness which shall never be theirs. He who hath wrought us to the self-same thing will secure that blessing to us for which he hath prepared us. The faintest impress of the seal of the Spirit is a better attestation of our part and lot with the people of God than all the presumptuous inferences which self-conceit can draw from its heated fancies.

Nor is the holy Spirit only the seal of the inheritance, he is also the earnest of it. Now an earnest is a part of the thing itself, given as a guarantee that the remainder will be forthcoming in due season. If a man is paid a part of his six-days wage in the middle of the week, it is earnest-money. In this an earnest differs from a pledge, for a pledge is returned when we receive that which is secured; but an earnest is not returned, for it is a part of that which is promised. Even so the

Holy Spirit is himself a great portion of the inheritance of the saints; and in having him we have the beginning perfectness, of heaven, of eternal glory. He is everlasting life, and his gifts, graces, and workings are the first principles of endless felicity. In having the holy Ghost we have the kingdom which it is our Father's good pleasure to give to his chosen.

This will be made clear by a few moments' reflection. Heaven will much consist in holiness; and it is clear that, as far as the Holy Ghost makes us holy here, he has implanted the beginnings of heaven. Heaven is victory; and each time that we overcome sin, Satan, the world, and the flesh, we have foretastes of the unfading triumph which causes the waving of palms in the new Jerusalem. Heaven is an endless Sabbath; and how can we have better antepasts of the perfect rest than by that joy and peace which are shed abroad in us by the Holy Ghost? Communion with God is a chief ingredient in the bliss of the glorified; and here below, by the Spirit of God, we are enabled to delight ourselves in the Lord, and rejoice in the God of our salvation. Fellowship with the Lord Jesus in all his gracious designs and purposes, and likeness to him in love to God and man, are also chief constituents in our perfected condition before the throne; and these the Spirit of holiness is working in us from day to day. To be pure in heart so as to see God, to be established in character so as to be fixed in righteousness, to be strong in good so as to overcome all evil, and to be cleansed from self so as to find our all in God; are not these, when carried to the full, among the central benedictions of the beatific vision? And are they not already bestowed upon us by that Spirit of glory and of power which even now rests upon us? It is so. In the Holy Spirit we have the things we seek after. In him the flower of heaven has come to us in the bud, the dawn of the day of glory has smiled upon us.

We are not, then, such strangers to the promised blessings as common talk would make us out to be. Many repeat, like parrots, the word, "Eye hath not seen, nor ear heard, neither have entered into the heart of man, the things which God hath prepared for them that love him" (I Cor. 2:9); but they fail to add the words which follow in the same Scripture, "but God hath revealed them unto us by his Spirit." What cruelty thus to cut the living child of Scripture in halves! The Holy Spirit has revealed to us what neither eye nor ear has perceived: he has drawn back the curtains, and bidden us see the secrets hidden from ages and from generations. Behold, in the life of God within your soul, the everlasting life which is promised to them that love God. The life of glory is but the continuance and the outgrowth of the life of grace. Behold, in reconciliation through the atoning blood, that celestial peace which is the groundwork of eternal rest. See, in the love of God shed abroad in the believing soul, a foretaste of the fragrance of felicity. Mark, in the immovable security and hallowed serenity of full assurance, a forecast of the infinite repose of Paradise. When our inward joys swell high, and burst into a song, then we hear preludes of the heavenly hallelujahs. If we would know the clusters of Canaan, lo, they are brought to us by those emotions and anticipations, which, under the guidance of the Spirit, have gone, like spies, into the good land, and brought us hence its choicest fruits!

It is not only that we *shall* have an inheritance: but WE HAVE IT. In having the Holy Spirit, we are already put in possession of the land which floweth with milk and honey. "We which have believed do enter into rest" (Heb. 4:3). "Ye are come unto mount Sion, and unto the city of the living God, and to an innumerable company of angels" (Heb. 12:22).

What remains for such persons, thus made partakers of a divine inheritance in the Son of God, but that they walk worthy of their high, holy, heavenly calling? "If ye then be risen with Christ, seek those things which are above, where Christ sitteth on the right hand of God" (Col. 3:1).

XX.

JESUS AND THE PROMISES

"For all the promises of God in him are yea, and in him Amen, unto the glory of God by us." II Cor. 1:20

JESUS, our Lord, stands for ever connected with the way of the promise. Indeed, he is "the way, the truth, and the life." No man comes to the Faithful Promiser but by Jesus Christ. We could not close this little book without a short chapter upon HIM. Our hope is that the reader will not attempt to obtain any comfort from a word that we have written, or even from the Word of God itself, except as he receives it through Jesus Christ. Apart from him the Scripture itself contains nothing which the soul of man may live upon. This, indeed, is the great fault of many—they search the Scriptures, for in them they think they have eternal life, but they will not come unto christ, that they might have life. Let us not be of this foolish company; but let us come to Jesus day by day knowing that it pleased the Father that in him should all fullness dwell. Only as we know him do we know the light, life, and liberty of the heirs of promise; and, as surely as we wander from him we roam into bondage. Oh, for grace to abide in him, that we may possess all the good things of the covenant made with us in him!

Jesus is the Gate of the promises. Through him the Lord is able to enter into gracious engagements with guilty men. Until "the seed of the woman" had been appointed to be the Mediator between God and man, no messages of comfort could be sent to the offending race. God had no word for sinners till the Word of God undertook to be made flesh, and to dwell among us. God could not communicate his mind of love to men except through Jesus, the Word. As God could not come to us apart from the Messenger of the covenant, so we could not approach to him except through the Mediator. Our fears drive us away from the Holy One till we see in the Son of God a Brother full of tender sympathy. The glory of the divine Trinity overawes us until we behold the milder radiance of the Incarnate God. We come to God through the humanity of his Son, and especially through that humanity suffering and dying on our behalf.

Jesus is the Sum of all the promises. When God promised his Son to be ours, he gave us in him all things necessary for our salvation. Every good gift and every perfect gift will be found within the person, offices, and work of our Redeemer. All the promises are "in him." If you would add them up, or make a long catalogue of all the blessings which they secure to us, you may save yourself the pains, and be happy to know that this is the full total—the Lord has given us his Son Jesus. As all the stars are in the sky, and all the waves are in the sea, so are all covenant blessings in Christ. We cannot think of a real blessing outside of our Lord: He is all in all. On this thread all pearls are strung: in this casket all gems are contained.

Jesus is the Guarantee of the promises. He that spared not his own son will deny nothing to his people. If he had ever thought of drawing back, he would have done so before he had made the infinite sacrifice of his Only-begotten Son. Never can there be a suspicion that the Lord will revoke any one of the promises since he has already fulfilled the greatest and most costly of them all. "How shall he not with him also freely give us all things?"

Jesus is the Confirmer of the promises. They are "in him yea, and in him Amen." His coming into our nature, his standing as our federal Head, and his fulfilling of all the stipulations of the covenant, have made all the articles of the divine compact firm and enduring. Now is it not only kind but just with God to keep his promises to men. Since Jesus has rendered, on man's behalf, a full recompense to the divine honour which sin has assailed, the justice of God unites with his love in securing the carrying out of every work of promise. As the rainbow is our assurance that Jesus our assurance that the floods of human sin shall never drown the faithful kindness of the Lord. He has magnified the law, and made it honourable; he must be rewarded for his soul-travail, and therefore all good things must come to those for whom he died. It would be an unhinging and dislocation of all things if the promises were now to become of none effect after our Lord has done all that was required to make them sure. If we are indeed one with the Lord Jesus Christ, the promises are as sure to us as the love of his Father is to him.

Jesus is the Rememberancer of the promises. He pleads with God on our behalf, and his plea is the divine promise. "He made intercession for the transgressors." For the good things which he has promised the Lord will be enquired of by us that he may do them for us; and that this enquiry may be carried out under the most encouraging circumstances, behold, the Lord Jesus himself becomes the Intercessor for us: for Zion's sake he doth not hold his peace, but day and night he makes remembrance of the everlasting covenant, and of the blood shereby it was sealed and ratified. At the back of every promise stands the living, pleading, and prevailing High-priest of our profession. We may forget the faithful promise, but he will not: he will present the incense of his merit, and the engagements of God on our behalf, in that place within the veil where he exercises omnipotent intercession.

Jesus is the Fulfiller of the promise. His first Advent brought us the major part of the blessings which the Lord has foreordained for his own, and his second Advent is to bring us the rest. Our spiritual riches are linked with his ever-adorable person. Because he lives, we live; because he reigns, we reign; because he is accepted, we are accepted. Soon, at his manifestation, we shall be manifested; in his triumph, we shall triumph; in his glory, we shall be glorified. He is himself the Alpha and the Omega of the promises of God: in him we have found life as sinners, in him we shall find glory as saints. If he be not risen, our hope is a delusion; but, since he has risen from the dead, we are justified; since he will come in the glory of the Father, we also shall be glorified.

READER, WHAT HAST THOU TO DO WITH CHRIST?

All will depend upon thine answer to this question? Dost thou rest alone in HIM? Then the Lord has promised to bless thee, and do thee good; and he will surprise thee with the amazing manner in which he will do this unto thee. *Nothing is too good for the Father to give to the man who delights in his Son Jesus.*

On the other hand, art thou trusting to thine own doings, feeling, prayings, and ceremonials? Then thou are of the works of the law, and thou art under the curse. See what we said of the seed of Hagar, the bondwoman; and guess what thy portion will be. Oh, that thou wouldst quit the house of bondage, and flee to the home of free grace, and become one whom God will bless

ACCORDING TO THE PROMISE!

God grant this great favour unto thee for the Lord Jesus Christ's sake!   Amen.

ORDER FORM

ORDERS MAY BE PLACED BY PHONE OR MAIL TO:

JIM OLIVER

P.O. BOX 241362

MONTGOMERY, AL 36124-1362

TELEPHONE (334) 396-2236

NAME____

ADDRESS____

CITY__________________________STATE______ZIP __________

TELEPHONE (________)_______________

COST OF BOOK: $15.99

SHIPPING AND HANDLING: $1.00 PER BOOK

$2.00 FOR 2 OR MORE BOOKS

TAX: 8% FOR ALABAMA RESIDENTS

ORDER FORM

ORDERS MAY BE PLACED BY PHONE OR MAIL TO:

JIM OLIVER

P.O. BOX 241362

MONTGOMERY, AL 36124-1362

TELEPHONE (334) 396-2236

NAME____

ADDRESS____

CITY__________________________STATE______ZIP __________

TELEPHONE (________)_______________

COST OF BOOK: $15.99

SHIPPING AND HANDLING: $1.00 PER BOOK

$2.00 FOR 2 OR MORE BOOKS